A EE I O OO

EASILY PRONOUNCED

ITALIAN

BY CLIFF LEAL DAVIS

Betty Chapman, President
EPLS PUBLISHING
631 N. Stephanie Street, Suite 398
Henderson, NV 89014
(702) 387-7220

ISBN 0-9728160-4-6

ACKNOWLEDGMENTS

Priscilla Leal Bailey, Senior Series Editor

EPLS has been extensively field-tested to reflect how foreign languages are actually used by contemporary native-speakers and all languages are endorsed by certified language consultants.

Italian Language Consultant Lucia Colazio

Special Thanks to Michael A. Curcio

Cover Design Clyde Peters

Maps courtesy of www.theodora.com/maps
Used with permission

Printed in the United States

10 9 8 7 6 5 4 3

INTRODUCTION

EASILY PRONOUNCED phrase books have been developed with the conviction that learning to speak a foreign language should be fun and easy.

The EPLS Vowel Symbol System is a revolutionary phonetic tool which stresses consistency, clarity and above all, simplicity! The basic vowel symbols are located on page seven for easy reference.

You will be amazed at how confidence in your pronunciation leads to an eagerness to talk to other people in their own language.

CONTENTS

Essential Words and Phrases / 10

Arrival / 52

Getting Around / 58

Hotel Survival / 70

Restaurant Survival / 82

Shopping / 106

Health / 114

General Information / 120

Dictionary / 128

Thanks...154

PRONUNCIATION GUIDE

Most English speakers are familiar with the Italian word Pizza. This is how its correct pronunciation would be represented in this system.

P(EE)́T-S(ah)

All Italian vowel sounds are assigned a specific non changing symbol. When these symbols are used in conjunction with consonants and read normally, pronunciation of even the most difficult foreign word becomes incredibly EASY.

On the following page you will find all the symbols used in this book. They are EASY to LEARN since their sounds are familiar. Beneath each symbol are three English words which contain the sound of the symbol.

THE SAME BASIC SYMBOLS ARE USED IN ALL EASY TO PRONOUNCE PHRASE BOOKS!

EPLS VOWEL SYMBOLS

(A)

Ace
Bake
Safe

(EE)

See
Green
Feet

(I)

Ice
Kite
Pie

(O)

Oak
Cold
Phone

(oo)

Cool
Pool
Too

(ĕ)

Pet
Red
Bed

(ah)

Rock
Hot
Off

(ow)

Cow
How
Now

EPLS CONSONANTS

Consonants are letters like T, D, and K. They are easy to recognize and their pronunciation seldom changes. The following pronunciation guide letters represent some unique Italian consonant sounds.

Ḇ	represents a slightly rolled r sound
Ḇ	represents a strongly rolled r sound
TS	represents the letter z in Italian. Pronounce the word hits without the hi or simply say pizza!
KY	pronounce like the c in cute
CH	pronounce like the ch in chair

PRONUNCIATION TIPS

- Each pronunciation guide word is broken into syllables. Read each word slowly, one syllable at a time, increasing speed as you become more familiar with the system.

- In Italian it is important to emphasize certain syllables. This mark (') over the syllable reminds you to stress that syllable.

- Most symbols are pronounced the way they look!

- Pronunciation and word choices in this book were chosen for their simplicity and effectiveness.

ESSENTIAL WORDS AND PHRASES

Here are some basic words and phrases that will help you express your needs and feelings in Italian.

Hello

Buon giorno

BWON JOB-NO

How are you?

Come sta?

KO-ME STah

Fine/ Very well

Molto bene

MOL-TO BE-NE

And you?

E lei?

E LE-EE

Goodbye

Arrivederci

ah-REE-VE-DER-CHEE

Good morning

Buon giorno

BWON   JOB-NO

Good evening

Buona sera

BWO-Nah   SE-Bah

Good night

Buona notte

BWO-Nah   NOT-Te

Mr.

Signor

SEEN-YOB

Mrs.

Signora

SEEN-YO-Bah

Miss

Signorina

SEEN-YO-BEE-Nah

Yes

Sí

SⒺⒺ

No

No

NⓄ

Please

Per piacere / Per favore

PⒺR   PⒺⒺ-ⓐⓗ-CHⒺ'-RⒺ

PⒺR   Fⓐⓗ-VⓄ'-RⒺ

Always remember to say please and thank you.

Thank you

Grazie

GRⓐⓗ'-TSⒺⒺ-Ⓔ

Excuse me

Mi scusi

MⒺⒺ   SKⓄⓄ'-ZⒺⒺ

I'm sorry

Mi dispiace

MⒺⒺ   DⒺⒺS-PⒺⒺ-ⓐⓗ'-CHⒺ

I'm a tourist

Sono un turista

SŌ-NO ᴓN TOO-RĒS-Tah

I don't speak Italian

Non parlo Italiano

NON Pah'R-LO ĒE-Tah-LĒE-ah'-NO

I speak a little Italian

Parlo un poco Italiano

Pah'R-LO ᴓN PŌ'-KO

ĒE-Tah-LĒE-ah'-NO

Do you understand English?

Capisce l'inglese?

Kah-PĒE'-SHĕ LĒEN-GLĕ'-Sĕ

I don't understand!

Non capisco!

NON Kah-PĒE'S-KO

Please repeat

Ripeta per favore

RĒE-Pĕ'-Tah Pĕ'R Fah-VO'-Rĕ

FEELINGS

I want...
Voglio ..
VOL-YO...

I have...
Ho...
O...

I know
Lo so
LO SO

I don't know
Non lo so
NON LO SO

I like it
Mi piace
MEE PEE-ah-CHe

I don't like it
Non mi piace
NON MEE PEE-ah-CHe

I'm lost

Mi sono perduto (perduta for a female)

MEE SÓ-NO PĕR-DOO-TO (ah)

I'm in a hurry

Ho fretta

O FRĕT-Tah

I'm tired

Sono stanco/a

SÓ-NO STahN-KO (ah)

I'm ill

Sono ammalato (ammalata for a female)

SÓ-NO ahM-Mah-Lah-TO (ah)

I'm hungry

Ho fame

O Fah-Mĕ

I'm thirsty

Ho sete

O Sĕ-Tĕ

I'm angry

Sono adirato

SÓ-NO ah-DEE-Rah-TO

INTRODUCTIONS

My name is...
Mi chiamo...

MEE KEE-ah'-MO...

What's your name?
Come si chiama?

KO'-ME SEE KEE-ah'-Mah

Where are you from?
Di dov'è Lei?

DEE DO-VE' LE'-EE

Do you live here?
Lei abita qui?

LE'-EE' ah-BEE-Tah KWEE

I just arrived
Sono appena arrivato

SO'-NO ahP-PE'-Nah ah-BEE-Vah'-TO

What hotel are you [staying] at?
In quale hotel sta?

EEN KWah'-LE O-TE'L STah

I'm at the...hotel

Sono all' hotel...

SŌ-NŌ ⓐL Ō-TⓔL....

It was nice to meet you

E' stato un piacere incontrarla

ⓔ STⓐ-TŌ ⓞN

PⒺ-ⓐ-CHⓔ-Rⓔ

ⒺN-KŌN-TRⓐR-Lⓐ

See you next time

Arrivederci a presto

ⓐ-RⒺ-Vⓔ-DⓔR-CHⒺ

ⓐ PRⓔS-TŌ

See you later

A piu tardi

ⓐ PⒺ-ⓞ Tⓐ R-DⒺ

So long!

Arrivederci

ⓐ-RⒺ-Vⓔ-DⓔR-CHⒺ

THE BIG QUESTIONS

Who?

Chi?

KEE

Who is it?

Chi è?

KEE   è

What?

Cosa?

KŌ-Zah

What's that?

Che cos'è quello?

Kè KŌ-Zè KWèL-LŌ

When?

Quando?

KWahN-DŌ

Where?

Dove?

DŌ-Vè

Where is...?

Dov'è...?

DO-Vě...

Which?

Quale?

KWah-Lě

Why?

Perchè?

PěR-Kě

How?

Come?

KO-Mě

How much? (money)

Quanto costa?

KWahN-TO KOS-Tah

How long?

Per quanto tempo?

PěR KWahN-TO TěM-PO

ASKING FOR THINGS

The following phrases are valuable when asking for directions, food or help, etc.

I would like...

Vorrei....

VO-Rẽ-EE...

I need...

Ho bisogno di...

O   BEE-ZON-YO   DEE...

Can you...

può...

PWO...

When asking for things be sure to say
please and thank you

Please

Per piacere

PẽR

PEE-ah-CHẽ-Rẽ

Thank you

Grazie

GRah-TSEE-ẽ

PHRASEMAKER

Combine I would like with the following phrases beneath it and you will have a good idea how to ask for things.

I would like...

Vorrei....

VO-Rē-EE...

---

more coffee

ancora del caffè

ahN-KO-Rah DēL Kah-Fē

---

some water

dell' acqua

DēL Lah-KWah

---

some ice

del ghiaccio

DēL GEE-ah-CHO

---

the menu

Il menù

EEL Mē-Noo

PHRASEMAKER

I need...

Ho bisogno...

Ⓞ BⒺⒺ-ZⓄN-YⓄ....

help

d'aiuto

Dⓐⓗ-YⓄⓄ-TⓄ

directions

di indicazioni

DⒺⒺ ⒺⒺN-DⒺⒺ-Kⓐⓗ-TSⒺⒺ-Ⓞ-NⒺⒺ

more money

di più soldi

DⒺⒺ PⒺⒺ-ⓄⓄ SⓄL-DⒺⒺ

change

di moneta

DⒺⒺ MⓄ-NⒺ-Tⓐⓗ

a lawyer

di un avvocato

DⒺⒺ ⓄⓄN ⓐⓗV-VⓄ-Kⓐⓗ-TⓄ

PHRASEMAKER

Can you...

può...

PWⓄ...

---

help me?

aiutarmi?

ⓐ-Yⓞⓞ-Tⓐ'R-MⒺⒺ

---

show me?

indicarmi?

ⒺⒺN-DⒺⒺ-Kⓐ'R-MⒺⒺ

---

give me...?

darmi...?

Dⓐ'R-MⒺⒺ

---

tell me...?

dirmi...?

DⒺ'R-MⒺⒺ

---

take me to...?

portarmi al...?

PⓄR-Tⓐ'R-MⒺⒺ ⓐL...

ASKING THE WAY

No matter how independent you are, sooner or later you'll probably have to ask directions.

Where is...?

Dov'è?

DO-Vĕ...

Is it near?

E' vicino?

ĕ VEE-CHEE-NO

Is it far?

E' lontano?

ĕ LON-Tah-NO

I'm lost!

Mi sono perduto (perduta for a female)

MEE SO-NO PĕR-DOO-TO (ah)

I'm looking for...

Sto cercando...

STO CHĕR-Kah-N-DO...

PHRASEMAKER

Where is...
Dov'è...
DŌ-Vĕ́...

the restroom?
la toilette?
Lah TWah-Lĕ́T

the telephone?
il telefono?
ĒL Tĕ-Lĕ́-FŌ-NŌ

the beach?
la spiaggia?
Lah SPĒ-ah́-Jah

the hotel...?
l' hotel...?
LŌ-Tĕ́L

the train for...?
il treno per...?
ĒL TRĕ́-NŌ Pĕ́R...

TIME

What time is it?
Che ora è?

Kĕ   Ó-Rah   ĕ

Morning
Mattino

Mah T-TEÉ-NO

Noon
Mezzogiorno

Mĕ-TSO-JÓB-NO

Night
Notte

NOÍT-Tĕ

Today
Oggi

Ó-JEE

Tomorrow
Domani

DO-Mahé-NEE

This week
Questa settimana
KWĕS-Tah Sĕt-Tee-Mah-Nah

This month
Questo mese
KWĕS-To Mĕ-Sĕ

This year
Questa' anno
KWĕ-STah ahN-No

Now
Adesso
ah-Dĕs-So

Soon
Presto
PRĕS-To

Later
Più tardi
Pee-oo Tah-R-Dee

Never
Mai
Mah-ee

WHO IS IT?

I

io

ⒺⒺ-Ⓞ

You (Formal)	Informal)
Lei	tu
LⒺ-ⒺⒺ	TⓄⓄ
Use this form of you with people you don't know well	Use this form of you with people you know well

We

Noi

NⓄⓎ

They

loro

LⓄ-ⓇⓄ

THE, A (AN), AND SOME

To use the correct form of The, A (An), or Some, you must know if the Italian word is masculine or feminine. Often you will have to guess! If you make a mistake, you will still be understood.

The

il, lo, l'

Ⓔ𝔼L/LⓄ/L

The before a singular masculine noun
(il) man is handsome

i, gli

Ⓔ𝔼/LYⒺ𝔼

The before a plural masculine noun
(i) men are handsome

La

Lⓐⓗ

The before a singular feminine noun
(la) woman is pretty

i, le

Ⓔ𝔼/Lⓔ

The before a plural feminine noun
(i) women are pretty

A or An

un / uno

ⓄⓄN / ⓄⓄ-NⓄ

A or **an** before a masculine noun
He is (un) man

una / un'

ⓄⓄN-ⓐⓗ / ⓄⓄN

A or **an** before a feminine noun
She is (una) woman

Some

Qualche

KWⓐⓗL-Kⓔ

Some before masculine and feminine nouns

ON THE PHONE

Placing phone calls in a foreign country can be a test of will and stamina! Besides the obvious language barriers, service can vary greatly from one town to the next.

- If you have a choice do not call from your hotel room. Service charges can add a hefty amount to your bill.

- In Italy, phone calls can be made from the post office, especially long distance calls.

KEY WORDS

Telephone
Telefono

Tĕ-Lĕ-FO-NO

Information
Informazione

EEN-FOR-Mah-TSEE-O-Nĕ

Operator
Signorina / Centralino

SEEN-YO-REE-Nah /
CHĕN-TRah-LEE-NO

Phone book
Guida telefonica

GWEE-Dah TĕLĕ-FO-NEE-Kah

Public telephone
Telefono pubblico

TĕLĕ-FO-NO POOB-BLEE-KO

May I use your telephone?

Posso usare il suo telefono?

PO'S-SO   oo-Zah'-Re

EEL   Soo'-O   Te-Le'-FO-NO

I don't speak Italian

Non parlo Italiano

NON   Pah'R-LO   EE-Tah-LEE-ah'-NO

long distance

Internazionale

EEN-Te'R-Nah-TSEE-O-Nah'-Le

collect

a carico del destinatario

ah   Kah'-REE-KO

DeL   De'S-TEE-Nah-Tah'-REE-O

person to person

diretta con preavviso

DEE-Re'T-Tah   KON

PRe'-ahV-VEE'-ZO

I want to call (this number)...

Vorrei chiamare questo numero...

VO-R**ĕ**́-EE KEE-ah-M**ah**́-R**ĕ**
KW**ĕ**́S-T**O** N**oo**-M**ĕ**́-R**O**...

1 uno **oo**́-N**O**	**2** due D**oo**́-**ĕ**	**3** tre TR**ĕ**
4 quattro KW**ah**́-TR**O**	**5** cinque CH**ĕ**́N-KW**ĕ**	**6** sei S**Ă**́-EE
7 sette S**ĕ**́T-T**ĕ**	**8** otto **O**́T-TO	**9** nove N**O**́-V**ĕ**
✳	**0** zero TS**ĕ**́-R**O**	#

AT THE POST OFFICE

Where is the post office?
Dov'è l'ufficio postale?

DO-Vĕ́ LOO-FĔÉ-CHO POS-Tah́-Lĕ

What time does the post office open?
A che ore apre l'ufficio postale?

ah Kĕ O-Rĕ ah-PRĕ
LOO-FĔÉ-CHO POS-Tah́-Lĕ

PHRASEMAKER

I need...

Ho bisogno di...

Ⓞ BⒺⒺ-ZⓄ'N-YⓄ DⒺⒺ...

stamps

francobolli

FRⓐⓗN-KⓄ-BⓄ'L-LⒺⒺ

an envelope

una busta

ⓄⓄ'-Nⓐⓗ BⓄⓄ'S-Tⓐⓗ

a pen

una penna

ⓄⓄ'-Nⓐⓗ PⒺ'N-Nⓐⓗ

AT THE BANK

As a traveler in a foreign country your primary contact with banks will be to exchange money.

- Have your passport handy when changing money.

- Change enough funds before leaving home to pay for tips, food and transportation to your final destination.

- Generally, you will receive a better rate of exchange at a bank, but rates can change from bank to bank.

- Current exchange rates are posted in bank and published daily in city newspapers.

- The Euro is the new "single currency" of the European Monetary Union and Italy is a participating nation.

KEY WORDS

Bank
Banca
BahN-Kah

Exchange office
Ufficio di cambio
oo-FEE-CHO DEE KahM-BEE-O

Money
Denaro
DĕE-Nah-RO

Money order
Mandato di pagamento
MahN-Dah-TO DEE Pah-Gah-MĕN-TO

Travelers checks
Travelers check
TRah-Vĕ-LĕRS CHĕK

Where is the bank?

Dov'è la banca?

DO-VĕÉ Lah Bah'N-Kah

What time does the bank open?

A che ore apre la banca?

ah Kĕ Ó-Rĕ ah-PRĕ
Lah Bah'N-Kah

Where is the Exchange Office?

Dov'è l'ufficio di cambio?

DO-VĕÉ Loo-FĒÉ-CHO
DĒ Kah'M-BĒ-O

What time does the
exchange office open?

A che ora apre l'ufficio di cambio?

ah Kĕ Ó-Rah ah-PRĕ
Loo-FĒÉ-CHO DĒ Kah'M-BĒ-O

Can I change dollars here?

Posso cambiare i dollari qui?

POS-SO Kah'M-BĒ-ah-Rĕ ĒE
DOL-Lah-RĒ KWĒ

Can you change this?

Puo' cambiarmi questo?

PWO KahM-BEE-ahB-MEE KWeS-TO

What is the exchange rate?

Qual'è il cambio?

KWah-Le EL KahM-BEE-O

I would like large bills

Vorrei banconote di grosso taglio

VO-Be-EE BahN-KO-NO-Te DEE
GBOS-SO TahL-YO

I need change

Ho bisogno moneta riccola

O BEE-ZON-YO MO-Ne-Te
BEE-KO-Lah

SIGHTSEEING &
ENTERTAINMENT

In most towns in Italy you will find tourist
information offices. Here you can usually obtain
brochures, maps, historical information, bus and
train schedules.

KEY WORDS

Admission
Entrata
ĕN-TRah-Tah

Map
Cartina
KahR-TEE-Nah

Reservation
Prenotazione
PRĕ-NO-Tah-TSEE-O-Nĕ

Ticket
Biglietto
BEEL-Yĕ'T-TO

Tour
Viaggio / Gita
VEE-ah-JO / JEE-Tah

Tour guide
Guida turistica
GWEE-Dah TOO-REES-TEE-Kah

Where is the tourist office?

Dov'è l'ufficio del turistico?

DO-Vẽ́ LOO-FẼ́-CHO DẼL
TOO-RẼ́S-TẼ-KO

Is there a tour to...?

Avete un giro turistico per...?

ah-Vẽ́-Tẽ OON JẼ-RO
TOO-RẼ́S-TẼ-KO PẼR...

Where do I buy a ticket?

Dove posso comprare un biglietto per...

DÓ-Vẽ PÓS-SO KOM-PRah́-Rẽ
OON BẼL-Yẽ́-TO PẼR...

How much does the tour cost?

Quanto costa il giro turistico?

KWah́N-TO KÓS-Tah ẼL JẼ́-RO
TOO-RẼ́S-TẼ-KO

How long does the tour take?

Quanto dura il giro turistico?

KWah́N-TO DOO-Rah ẼL
JẼ́-RO TOO-RẼ́S-TẼ-KO

PHRASEMAKER

Where can I find...

Dove posso trovare...

DŌ-Vĕ PŌS-SO TRŌ-Vah-Rĕ

a golf course?

un campo da golf?

ⓄⓄN Kah́M-PⓄ Dah GⓄLF

a health club?

un club ginnico?

ⓄⓄN KLⓄⓄB JEE̋N-NEÉ-KⓄ

a swimming pool?

una piscina?

ⓄⓄ-Nah PEE-SHEÉ-Nah

a tennis court?

un campo da tennis?

ⓄⓄN Kah́M-PⓄ Dah TĕN-NEES

USEFUL OPPOSITES

Near	**Far**
vicino	lontano
VEE-CHEE-NO	LON-Tah-NO

Here	**There**
Qui	Là
KWEE	Lah

Left	**Right**
Sinistra	Destra
SEE-NEES-TRah	DeS-TRah

A little	**A lot**
Un poco	Molto
OON PO-KO	MOL-TO

More	**Less**
Di più	Meno
DEE PEE-OO	Me-NO

Big	**Small**
Grande	Piccolo
GRahN-De	PeK-KO-LO

Opened	**Closed**
Aperto	Chiuso
@ah-P@R-T@	KY@-Z@

Clean	**Dirty**
Pulito	Sporco
P@-L@-T@	SP@R-K@

Good	**Bad**
Buono	Cattivo
BW@-N@	K@T-T@-V@

Vacant	**Occupied**
Libero	Occupato
L@-B@-R@	@-K@-P@-T@

Right	**Wrong**
Giusto	Sbagliato
J@S-T@	SB@L-Y@-T@

WORDS OF ENDEARMENT

I love you

Ti amo

TEE ah-MO

My love

Amore mio

ah-MO-REe MEE-O

My life

Vita mia

VEE-Tah MEE-ah

My friend (to a male)

Amico mio

ah-MEE-KO MEE-O

My friend (to a female)

Amica mia

ah-MEE-Kah MEE-ah

Kiss me!

Baciami!

Bah-CHah-MEE

WORDS OF ANGER

What do you want?
Che cosa vuole?
Kĕ KŌ-Zah VWŌ-Lĕ?

Leave me alone!
Mi lasci in pace!
MEE Lah-SHEE EEN Pah-CHĕ

Go away!
Vada via!
Vah-Dah VEE-ah

Stop bothering me!
Non mi stia a seccare!
NON MEE STEE-ah ah SĕK-Kah-Rĕ

Be Quiet!
silenzio!
SEE-LĕN-TSEE-O

That's enough!
Basta!
Bah S-Tah

COMMON EXPRESSIONS

When you are at a loss for words but have the feeling you should say something, try one of these!

Who knows?

Chi lo sa?

K(EE) L(O) S(ah)

That's the truth!

E' la verità!

(ĕ) L(ah) V(ĕ)-R(EE)-T(ah)

Sure!

Sicuro!

S(EE)-K(oo)-R(O)

Wow!

Che sorpresa!

K(ĕ) S(O)R-PR(ĕ)-Z(ah)

What's happening?

Che cosa succede?

K(ĕ) K(O)-Z(ah) S(oo)-CH(ĕ)-D(ĕ)

I think so!

Penso di sí!

P(ĕ)N-S(O) D(EE) S(EE)

Cheers!

Salute!

S@h-L@-T@

Good luck!

Buona fortuna!

BW@-N@h F@R-T@-N@h

With pleasure!

Con piacere!

K@N P@-@h-CH@-R@

My goodness!

Per l'amor del cielo!

P@R L@h-M@R D@L CH@-L@

What a shame or Thats too bad!

Peccato

P@K-K@h-T@

Well done! Bravo!

Bene! / Bravo!

B@-N@ / BR@h-V@

USEFUL COMMANDS

Stop!
Alt !

@LT

Go!
Forza!

FÓR-TS@

Wait!
Aspetti!

@-SPĔT-TEE

Hurry!
Ho fretta

O   FRĔT-T@

Slow down!
Rallenti!

R@L-LĔN-TEE

Come here!
Venga qui!

VĔN-G@   KWEE

Help!
Aiuto!

@-YOO-TO

EMERGENCIES

Fire!

Al fuoco!

ⓐL FWⓄ-K Ⓞ

Emergency!

Emergenza!

ⓔ-MⓔB-JⓔN-TSⓐ

Call the police!

Chiamate la polizia!

KⒺⒺ-ⓐ-Mⓐ-Tⓔ Lⓐ PⓄ-LⒺⒺ-TSⒺⒺ-ⓐ

Call a doctor!

Chiamate un medico!

KⒺⒺ-ⓐ-Mⓐ-Tⓔ ⓄⓄN Mⓔ-DⒺⒺ-KⓄ

Call an ambulance!

Chiamate un' ambulanza.!

KⒺⒺ-ⓐ-Mⓐ-Tⓔ ⓄⓄN

ⓐM-BⓄⓄ-Lⓐ'N-TSⓐ

I need help

Ho bisogno d'aiuto

Ⓞ BⒺⒺ-ZⓄN-YⓄ Dⓐ-YⓄⓄ-TⓄ

ARRIVAL

Passing through customs should be easy since there are usually agents available who speak English. You may be asked how long you intend to stay and if you have anything to declare.

- Have your passport ready.

- Be sure all documents are up to date.

- While in a foreign country, it is wise to keep receipts for everything you buy.

- Be aware that many countries will charge a departure tax when you leave. Your travel agent should be able to find out if this affects you.

- If you have connecting flights, be sure to reconfirm them in advance.

- Make sure your luggage is clearly marked inside and out.

- Take valuables and medicines in carry on bags.

KEY WORDS

Baggage
Bagaglio
Bah-Gah'L-Yo

Customs
Dogana
Do-Gah'-Nah

Documents
Documenti
Do-Koo-Mē'N-Tee

Passport
Passaporto
Pah'S-Sah-Po'R-To

Porter
Facchino
Fah-Kee'-No

Tax
Imposta
EEM-Po'S-Tah

USEFUL PHRASES

I have nothing to declare

Non ho nulla da dichiarare

NON O NOOL-Lah Dah
DEE-KEE-ah-Rah-Re

I'm here on business

Sono in viaggio d'affari

SO-NO EEN VEE-ah-JO DahF-Fah-REE

I'm here on vacation

Sono in vacanza

SO-NO EEN Vah-Kah'N-TSah

Here is my passport

Ecco (il mio) passaporto

e-KO EEL MEE-O
PahS-Sah-POB-TO

Is there a problem?

Ci sono dei problema?

CHEE SO-NO De-EE
PRO-BLe-Mah

PHRASEMAKER

I'll be staying...

Resterò qui...

Rĕs-Tĕ́-Rō KWĔĒ...

one week

una settimana

ŌṒ-Nah SĔ́T-TĒĒ-Mah́-Nah

two weeks

due settimana

Dŏŏ́-ĕ̃ SĔ́T-TĒĒ-Mah́-Nah

one month

un mese

ŌŌN MĔ́-Sĕ̃

two months

due mesi

Dŏŏ́-ĕ̃ MĔ́-SĒĒ

I need a porter!

Ho bisogno di Facchino!

Ⓞ BEE-ZOʹN-YⓄ DEE Fⓐh-KEEʹ-NⓄ

These are my bags

Queste sono le mie valigia

KWEʹS-Tĕ SOʹ-NⓄ Lĕ
MEEʹ-ĕ Vⓐh-LEEʹ-Jⓐh

I'm missing a bag

Mi manca una valigia

MEE MⓐhʹN-Kⓐh ⓄⓄ-Nⓐh Vⓐh-LEEʹ-Jⓐh

Take my bags to a taxi please

Per favore porti le mie valigia al tassì

PĕR Fⓐh-VOʹ-Rĕ POʹR-TEE Lĕ
MEEʹ-ĕ Vⓐh-LEEʹ-CHⓐh ⓐhL TⓐhS-SEE

Thank you. This is for you

Grazie. Questo eʹ per lei

GRⓐhʹ-TSEE-ĕ
KWEʹS-TⓄ ĕ PĕR Lĕ-EE

PHRASEMAKER

Where is...

Dov'è?

D⊙-V⑊́...

customs?

Dogana?

D⊙-Gⓐⓗ́-Nⓐⓗ

baggage claim?

iL ritiro bagagli?

ⒺⒺL RⒺⒺ-TⒺⒺ́-R⊙ Bⓐⓗ-Gⓐⓗ́-LⒺⒺ

the money exchange?

l'ufficio di cambio?

L⍟-FⒺⒺ́-CH⊙ DⒺⒺ Kⓐⓗ́M-BⒺⒺ-⊙

the taxi stand?

il posteggio dei taxi?

ⒺⒺL P⊙-STⓔ́-J⊙ Dⓔ TⓐⓗS-SⒺⒺ́

the bus stop?

la fermata dell' autobus?

Lⓐⓗ Fⓔ́R-Mⓐⓗ́-Tⓐⓗ DⓔL ⊚́-T⊙-B⍟S

GETTING AROUND

Getting around in a foreign country can be an adventure in itself! Taxi (FTASSI) and bus drivers do not always speak English, so it is essential to be able to give simple directions. The words and phrases in this chapter will help you get where you're going.

- Trains are used frequently by visitors to Europe. Schedules and timetables are easily understood. Arrive early to allow time for ticket purchasing and checking in and remember, trains leave on time!

- Check with your travel agent about special rail passes which allow unlimited travel within a set period of time.

KEY WORDS

Airport

Aeroporto

@ah-@ě-RO-PÓR-TO

Bus Station / Bus Stop

Stazione degli autobus
fermata dell' autobus

ST@ah-TS@EE-O'-N@ě D@ě-L@EE @ow-TO-B@ooS

F@ě-R-M@ah'-T@ah D@ěL @ow'-TO-B@ooS

Car Rental Agency

Agenzia di autonoleggio

@ah-J@ěN-TS@EE-Y@ah D@EE

@ow-TO-NO-L@ě'-CHO

Subway Station

Metropolitana

M@ě-TRO-PO-L@EE-T@ah'-N@ah

Taxi Stand

Posteggio di tassì

PO-ST@ě'-JO D@EE T@ahS-S@EE'

Train Station

Stazione ferroviaria

ST@ah-TS@EE-O'-N@ě F@ě-RO-V@EE-@ah'-R@EE-@ah

AIR TRAVEL

Arrivals
Arrivi

ah-BEE-VEE

Departures
Partenza

Pah-TEN-TSah

Flight number...
Numero di volo

Noo-MEE-RO DEE VO-LO

Airline
Compagnia aerea

KOM-Pah-NEE-ah ah-EE-REE-ah

The gate
Il cancello

EEL Kah-N-CHEE-L-LO

Information
Informazione

EEN-FOB-Mah-TSEE-O-NEE

Ticket (airline)
Biglietto aereo

BEEL-YEET-TO ah-EE-REE-O

Reservations
Prenotazione

PREE-NO-Tah-TSEE-O-NEE

PHRASEMAKER

I would like a seat...

Vorrei un posto...

VO-RĕE-EE OON POS-TO...

in the no smoking section

Tra i non fumatori

TRah EE NON FOO-Mah-TO-REE

next to the window

Accanto al finestrino

ahK-Kahn-TO ahL FEE-NĕS-TREE-NO

on the aisle

Vicino al corridoio

VEE-CHEE-NO ahL KO-REE-DO-EE-O

near the exit

Vicino all' uscita

VEE-CHEE-NO ahL OO-SHEE-Tah

BUS TRAVEL

Bus

autobus

ⓞⓌ-Tⓞ-BⓞⓞS

Where is the bus stop?

Dov'è la fermata dell' autobus?

Dⓞ-Vⓔ́ LⓐⒽ Fⓔ́R-MⓐⒽ-TⓐⒽ
Dⓔ́L ⓞⓌ-Tⓞ-BⓞⓞS

Do you go to...?

Va a...?

VⓐⒽ ⓐⒽ...

What is the fare?

Quanto costa il biglietto?

KWⓐⒽ́N-Tⓞ Kⓞ́S-TⓐⒽ
ⒺⒺL BⒺⒺL-Yⓔ́-Tⓞ

Do I need exact change?

Bisogno esatto moneta riccola

BⒺⒺ-Zⓞ́N-Yⓞ ⓔ́-SⓐⒽT-Tⓞ
Mⓞ-Nⓔ́-TⓐⒽ RⒺⒺK-Kⓞ́-LⓐⒽ

PHRASEMAKER

I would like a seat...
Vorrei un posto...
V◯-R◯-◯ ◯N P◯S-T◯...

in the no smoking section
Tra i non fumatori
TR◯ ◯ N◯N F◯-M◯-T◯-R◯

next to the window
Accanto al finestrino
◯K-K◯N-T◯ ◯L F◯-N◯S-TR◯-N◯

on the aisle
Vicino al corridoio
V◯-CH◯-N◯ ◯L K◯-R◯-D◯-◯-◯

near the exit
Vicino all' uscita
V◯-CH◯-N◯ ◯L ◯-SH◯-T◯

in first class
in prima classe
◯N PR◯-M◯ KL◯S-S◯

BY CAR

Fill it up
Faccia il pieno
Fẩ-CHẩ ẺL PẺ-ẻ́-Nⓞ

Please check...
Per piacere...Per favore
Pẽ́R PẼ-ẩ-CHẽ́-Rẽ̀...PF

the oil
l'olio
Lⓞ́-LⒺ-ⓞ

the battery
la batteria
Lẩ Bẩ̀T-Tẽ̀-RẺ́-ẩ

the tires
le gomme
Lẽ̀ Gⓞ́M-Mẽ̀

the water
l'acquai
Lẩ́-KWẩ-Ⓔ

the brakes
freni
FRẽ̀-NⒺ

Can you help me?

Può aiutarmi?

PWO ah-YOO-TahR-MEE

My car won't start

La mia auto non parte

Lah MEE-ah OW-TO NON PahR-Tĕ

I need a mechanic

Ho bisogno di un meccanico

O BEE-ZON-YO DEE
OON MĕK-Kah-NEE-KO

Can you fix it?

Può aggiustarla?

PWO ah-JOOS-TahR-Lah

What will it cost?

Quanto mi costerà?

KWahN-TO MEE KOS-Tĕ-Rah

How long will it take?

Quanto tempo ci vorrà?

KWahN-TO TĕM-PO
CHEE VOR-Rah

SUBWAYS AND TRAINS

Where is the subway station?

Dov'è la stazione della metropolitana?

DO-Vĕ́ Lah STah-TSEE-O-Nĕ
DĕL-Lah Mĕ-TRO-PO-LEE-Tah-Nah

Where is the train station?

Dov'è la stazione ferroviaria?

DO-Vĕ Lah STah-TSEE-O-Nĕ
Fĕ-RO-VEE-ah-REE-ah

A one way ticket please

Un biglietto d' andata, per favore

OON BEEL-Yĕ́T-TO Dah-Dah́-Tah PF

A round trip ticket

Un biglietto d' andata e ritorno

OON BEEL-Yĕ́-TO Dah-Dah́-Tah
ĕ REE-TOŔ-NO

First class

Prima classe

PREE-́Mah KLah́S-Sĕ

Second class

Seconda classe

Sĕ-KON-Dah KLah́S-Sĕ

Which train do I take to go to...

Quale treno devo prendere per andare a...

KWah-Lĕ TRĕ-NO Dĕ-VO

PRŏN-Dĕ-Rĕ PĕR ahN-Dah-Rĕ ah...

What is the fare?

Quanto costa il biglietto?

KWahN-TO KOS-Tah

EEL BEEL-YĕT-TO

Is this seat taken?

Questo posto è occupato?

KWĕS-TO POS-TO

ĕ O-Koo-Pah-TO

Do I have to change trains?

Devo cambiar treno?

Dĕ-VO KahM-BEE-ahR TRĕ-NO

Does this train stop at...?

Questo treno si ferma a...?

KWĕS-TO TRĕ-NO SEE

FĕR-Mah ah...

TAXI

Can you call a taxi for me?

Potrebbe chiamarmi un tassì?

PO-TREB-Be KEE-ah-MahB-MEE
ON TahS-SEE

Are you available?

E' libero?

e LEE-Be-RO

I want to go...

Vorrei andare...

VO-Re-EE ahN-Dah-Re...

Stop here please

Si fermi qui per favore

SEE FeB-MEE KWEE PF

Please wait

Mi aspetti per favore

MEE ah-SPeT-TEE PF

How much do I owe?

Quanto le devo?

KWahN-TO Le De-VO

PHRASEMAKER

I would like to go...

Vorrei andare...

VO-RÉ-EE ahN-Dah-RÉ...

to the hotel...

all' hotel...

ahL O-TÉL...

to this address

a questo indirizzo

ah KWÉS-TO EEN-DEE-REET-TSO

to the airport

all 'aeroporto

ahL ah-É-RO-PO'R-TO

to the subway station

alla stazione della metropolitana

ah-Lah STah-TSEE-O-NÉ DÉL-Lah
MÉ-TRO-PO-LEE-Tah-Nah

to the hospital

all' ospedale

ahL OS-PÉ-Dah-LÉ

HOTEL SURVIVAL

A wide selection of accommodations, ranging from the most basic to the most extravagant, are available wherever you travel in Italy. When booking your room, find out what amenities are included for the price you pay.

- Make reservations well in advance and get written confirmation of reservation before you leave home.

- Always have identification ready when checking in.

- Hotels in some foreign countries may require you to hand over your passport when checking in. It is usually returned the next day.

- Do not leave valuables, prescriptions or cash in your room when you are not there!

- Electrical items like blow dryers may need an adaptor. Your hotel may be able to provide one, but to be safe take one with you.

KEY WORDS

Hotel
H.otel
Ⓞ-TёّL

Bellman
Fattorino
FⓐT-TⓄ-RⒺⒺ-NⓄ

Maid
cameriera
Kⓐ-Mⓔّ-RⒺⒺ-ёّ-Rⓐ

Message
Messaggio
MёّS-Sⓐّ-JⓄ

Reservation
Prenotazione
PRёّ-NⓄ-Tⓐ-TSⒺⒺ-Óّ-Nёّ

Room service
Servizio in camera
SёّR-VⒺⒺّ-TSⒺⒺ-Ⓞ
ⒺⒺN Kⓐّ-Mёّ-Rⓐ

CHECKING IN

My name is... (I am...)

Mi chiamo...

MEE KEE-ah-MO...

I have a reservation

Ho la prenotazione

O Lah PRE-NO-Tah-TSEE-O-NE

Have you any vacancies?

Avete stanze libere?

ah-VE-TE STahN-TSE
LEE-BE-RE

What is the charge per night?

Quanto costa per notte?

KWahN-TO KOS-Tah
PER NOT-TE

Is there room service?

C'è il servizio in camera?

CHE EEL SER-VEE-TSEE-O
EEN Kah-ME-Rah

PHRASEMAKER

I would like a room with...

Vorrei una stanza con...

VO-Rḕ-EE ōō-Nah

STahŃ-TSah KON...

---

a bath

un bagno

ōoN BahŃ-YO

---

a shower

una doccia

ōō-Nah DO-CHah

---

one bed

un letto

ōoN LḕT-TO

---

two beds

due letti

Dōō-ḕ LḕT-TEE

---

a view

una vista

ōō-Nah VEEŚ-Tah

USEFUL PHRASES

Where is the dining room?

Dov'è la sala da pranzo?

DO-Vĕ Lah Sah-Lah
Dah PRahN-TSO

Are meals included?

I pasti sono inclusi?

EE PahS-TEE SO-NO
EEN-KLoo-ZEE

What time is...

A che ora è...

ah Kĕ O-Rah ĕ...

---

breakfast?

la colazione?

Lah KO-Lah-TSEE-O-Nĕ

---

lunch?

il pranzo?

EEL PRahN-TSO

---

dinner?

la cena?

Lah CHĕ-Nah

My room key please

La chiave per favore

Lah KEE-ah-Vě Pěʀ Fah-Vō-Rě

Are there any messages for me?

Ci sono de messaggi per me?

CHEE SŌ-NŌ Dě MěS-Sah-JEE Pěʀ Mě

Please wake me at...

Per favore mi svegli alle...

Pěʀ Fah-Vō-Rě MEE SVěL-YEE ah-L-Lě..

6:00
sei
Sě-EE

6:30
sei e mezzo
Sě-EE ě Mě-TSŌ

7:00
sette
SěꞱ-Tě

7:30
sette e mezzo
SěꞱ-Tě ě Mě-TSŌ

8:00
otto
ŌꞱ-TŌ

8:30
otto e mezzo
ŌꞱ-TŌ ě Mě-TSŌ

9:00
nove
NŌ-Vě

9:30
nove e mezzo
NŌ-Vě ě Mě-TSŌ

PHRASEMAKER

I need...

Ho bisogno...

Ⓞ BⒺⒺ-ZÓN-YⓄ...

soap

di sapone

DⒺⒺ Sⓐⓗ-PÓ-NⒺ̌

more towels

di altri asciugamani

DⒺⒺ ⓐⓗL-TRⒺⒺ

ⓐⓗ-SHⓄⓄ-Gⓐⓗ-Mⓐⓗ́-NⒺⒺ

ice cubes

di cubetti di ghiaccio

DⒺⒺ KⓄⓄ-BⒺ̌T-TⒺⒺ DⒺⒺ

GⒺⒺ-ⓐⓗ́-CHⓄ

toilet paper

di carta igienica

DⒺⒺ Kⓐⓗ́R-Tⓐⓗ ⒺⒺ-JⒺ̌-NⒺⒺ-Kⓐⓗ

a bellman
di un fattorino

DEE OON FAT-TO-REE-NO

a maid
di una cameriera

DEE OO-Nah KAH-MEE-REE-eh-Rah

the manager
del direttore

DEL DEE-RET-TO-RE

a babysitter
di una babysitter

DEE OO-Nah BE-BEE-SEE-TER

an extra key
di una chiave extra

DEE OO-Nah KEE-ah-VE EKS-TRah

a hotel safe
di una cassaforte

DEE OO-Nah KAH-SAH-FOR-TE

more blankets
di altre coperte

DEE AHL-TRE KO-PER-TE

PHRASEMAKER
(PROBLEMS)

There is no...

Manca...

Mah́N-Kah...

hot water

l'acqua calda

Lah́-KWah Kah́L-Dah

heat

il riscaldamento

EEL REES-Kah́L-Dah-Mě́N-TO

light

la luce

Lah LOo-CHě

electricity

la corrente

Lah KO-Rě́N-Tě

toilet paper

di carta igienica

DEE Kah́R-Tah EE-Jě-NEE-Kah

PHRASEMAKER
(SPECIAL NEEDS)

Do you have...

Avete...

ⓐ-Vⓔ́-Tⓔ...

---

facilities for the disabled?

accomodamenti per gli handicappati?

ⓐ-KⓄ-MⓄ-Dⓐ-Mⓔ́N-TⒺ Pⓔ́R
GLⒺ ⓐN-DⒺ-Kⓐ́P-Pⓐ́-TⒺ

---

a wheel chair?

una poltrona da invalido

ⓄⓄ́-Nⓐ PⓄL-TRⓄ́-Nⓐ
Dⓔ ⒺN-Vⓐ-LⒺ́-DⓄ

---

an elevator?

un ascensore?

ⓄⓄN ⓐ-SHⓔ́N-SⓄ́-Rⓔ

---

a ramp?

una rampa d'accesso?

ⓄⓄ́-Nⓐ Rⓐ́M-Pⓐ Dⓐ-CHⓔ́-SⓄ

CHECKING OUT

The bill please

Vorrei il conto per favore

V⊙-R͜ẽ-EE   EEL   K⊙N-T⊙   PF

Is this bill correct?

Questo conto è esatto?

KWẽS-T⊙   K⊙N-T⊙   ẽ   ẽ-Z͜ah͜T-T⊙

Do you accept credit cards?

Accettate carte di credito?

ah-CHẽ-T͜ah͜-Tẽ   K͜ah͜R-Tẽ
DEE   KRẽ-DEE-T⊙

Could you have my luggage brought down?

Potrebbe far portare giu' le mie valigia?

P⊙-TRẽ-Bẽ   F͜ah͜R   P⊙R-T͜ah͜-Rẽ
J͜oo͜   Lẽ   MEE-ẽ   V͜ah͜-LEE-CH͜ah͜

Can you call a taxi for me?

Potrebbe chiamarmi un tassì?

P⊙-TRẽB-Bẽ   KEE-ah-M͜ah͜R-MEE
oo͜N   T͜ah͜S-SEE

I had a very good time!

Ho passato dei giorni bellissimi!

Ⓞ Pⓐⓗ S-Sⓐⓗ'-Tⓞ Dⓔ JⓄ'R-Nⓔⓔ
Bⓔ̆L-Lⓔⓔ'S-Sⓔⓔ-Mⓔⓔ

Thanks for everything

Grazie di tutto

GRⓐⓗ'-TSⓔⓔ Dⓔⓔ Tⓞⓞ'T-Tⓞ

I'll see you next time

Arrivederci a presto

ⓐⓗ-Rⓔⓔ-Vⓔ̆-Dⓔ̆'R-CHⓔⓔ ⓐⓗ
PRⓔ̆'S-Tⓞ

Goodbye

Arrivederci

ⓐⓗ-Rⓔⓔ-Vⓔ̆-Dⓔ̆'R-CHⓔⓔ

RESTAURANT SURVIVAL

Italy is famous for its cuisine. You are encouraged to try all the regional specialties. This chapter will help you order foods you are familiar with.

- Breakfast (La Prima Colazione) is usually served at your hotel. Lunch (Il Pranzo) normally served from noon to 3:00 p.m., and dinner (La Cena) from 7 p.m. to 10 p.m.

SIGNS TO LOOK FOR:

BAR OR SNACK BAR

TRATTORIA (LOCAL DISHES)

PIZZERIA

RISTORANTE (FINE DINNING)

KEY WORDS

Breakfast

la colazione?

L@h KO-L@h-TSEE-O-N@

Lunch

il pranzo?

EEL PR@hN-TSO

Dinner

la cena?

L@h CH@-N@h

Waiter

Cameriere

K@h-M@-REE-@-R@

Waitress

Cameriera

K@h-M@-REE-@-R@h

Restaurant

Ristorante

REES-TO-R@hN-T@

USEFUL PHRASES

A table for...

Un tavolo per...

ⓞⓞN Tⓐⓗ-Vⓞ-Lⓞ Pⓔʀ...

2	4	6
due	quattro	sei
Dⓞⓞ-ⓔ	KWⓐⓗT-Tʀⓞ	Sⓔ-ⒺⒺ

The menu please

Il menù, per favore

ⒺⒺL Mⓔ-Nⓞⓞ PF

Separate checks please

Conti separati, per favore

KⓞN-TⒺⒺ Sⓔ-Pⓐⓗ-ʀⓐⓗ-TⒺⒺ PF

We are in a hurry

Siamo di fretta

SⒺⒺ-ⓐⓗ-Mⓞ DⒺⒺ FʀⓞT-Tⓐⓗ

What do you recommend?

Che cosa consiglia?

Kⓔ Kⓞ-Zⓐⓗ KⓞN-SⒺⒺL-Yⓐⓗ

Prease bring me...

Per favore, mi porti...

PĕR Fah-VO'-Rĕ MEE PO'R-TEE

Please bring us...

Per favore ci porti...

PĕR Fah-VO'-Rĕ CHEE PO'R-TEE

I'm hungry

Ho fame

O Fah'-Mĕ

I'm thirsty

Ho sete

O Sĕ'-Tĕ

Is service included?

Il servizio e incluso?

EEL SĕR-VEE'-TSEE-O

ĕ EEN-KLoo'-ZO

The bill please

Vorrei il conto per favore

VO-Rĕ'-EE EEL KO'N-TO PF

ORDERING BEVERAGES

Ordering beverages is easy and a great way to practice your Italian! In many foreign countries you will have to request ice with your drinks.

Please bring me...

Per favore, mi porti...

PĒR FⒶh-VⓄ-RĒ MⒺⒺ PⓄR-TⒺⒺ...

coffee...	**tea...**
del caffè	del tè
DĒL KⒶh-FⒺ	DĒL TⒺ

with cream

con panna

KⓄN PⒶN-NⒶh

with sugar

con zucchero

KⓄN TSⓄⓄ-KⒺ-RⓄ

with lemon

con limone

KⓄN LⒺⒺ-MⓄ-NⒺ

with ice

con ghiaccio

KⓄN GⒺⒺ-Ⓐh-CHⓄ

Soft drinks

Bibite

BEE-BEE-Tĕ

Milk

il Latte

EEL LahT-Tĕ

Hot chocolate

il Cioccolata

EEL CHOK-KO-Lah-Tah

Juice

Succo

TSOOK-KO

Orange juice

Succo di arancia

TSOO-KO DEE ah-RahN-CHah

Ice water

Acqua con ghiaccio

ah-KWah KON GEE-ah-CHO

Mineral water

Acqua minerale

ah-KWah MEE-Nĕ-Rah-Lĕ

AT THE BAR

Bartender

Barista

Bah-REE'S-Tah

The wine list please

La lista dei vini, per favore

Lah LEE'S-Tah Dĕ VEE-NEE PF

Cocktail

Cocktail

KOK-TĕL

On the rocks

Con ghiaccio

KON GEE-ah'-CHO

Straight

Senza ghiaccio

SĕN-TSah GEE-ah'-CHO

With lemon

con limone

KON LEE-MO'-Nĕ

PHRASEMAKER

I would like a glass of...
Vorrei un bicchiere di...
VO-Bĕ'-EE oON BEEK-Yĕ'-Bĕ DEE...

champagne
champagne
SHahM-Pah'N-Yah

beer
birra
BEE'R-Rah

wine
La lista dei vini, per favore
Lah LEE'S-Tah Dĕ VEE'-NEE PF

red wine
vino rosso
VEE'-NO ROS'-SO

white wine
vino bianco
VEE'-NO BEE-ah'N-KO

ORDERING BREAKFAST

In Italy breakfast, is usually small, consisting of a croissant or warm bread with butter and jam accompanied by café au lait, hot tea or hot chocolate.

Bread

Pane

P(ah)́-N(ĕ)

Toast

Pane tostato

P(ah)́-N(ĕ) T(O)S-T(ah)́-T(O)

---

with butter

con burro

K(O)N B(oo)́-R(O)

---

with jam

con marmellata

K(O)N M(ah)R-M(ĕ)L-L(ah)́-D(ah)

PHRASEMAKER

I would like...

Vorrei...

VO-Ŕē-EE...

two eggs...

due uovo...

DŌŌ-ĕ WŌ-VO

with bacon

con pancetta

KON PahN-CHē-Tah

with ham

con prosciutto

KON PRO-SHŌŌT-TO

with potatoes

con patate

KON Pah-Tah-Tē

LUNCH AND DINNER

Although you are encouraged to sample great Italian cuisine, it is important to be able to order foods you are familiar with. This section will provide words and phrases to help you.

I would like...

Vorrei....

VO-Rĕ-EE...

We would like...

Vorremmo...

VO-RĕM-MO...

Bring us...

Per favore ci porti...

PĕR Fah-VO-Rĕ CHEE POR-TEE

The lady would like...

La signora vorrebbe...

Lah SEEN-YO-Rah VO-RĕB-Bĕ...

The gentleman would like...

IL signori vorrebbe...

EEL SEEN-YO-REE VO-RĕB-Bĕ

STARTERS

Appetizers

Antipasti

@N-T℮℮-P@S-T℮℮

Bread and butter

Pane e burro

P@-N℮   ℮   B℮-R℮

Cheese

Formaggio

F℮R-M@-J℮

Fruit

frutta

FR℮T-T@

Salad

Insalata

℮N-S@-L@-T@

Soup

Zuppa

TS℮P-P@

MEATS

Beef

Manzo

M@N-TS⓪

Beef Steak

Bistecca

B㏒S-Tĕ́K-K@

Pork

Maiale

M@-Y@́-Lĕ

Ham

con prosciutto

K⓪N P℞⓪-SH⑩́T-T⓪

Bacon

con pancetta

K⓪N P@N-CHĕ́T-T@

Lamb

Agnello

@N-Yĕ́L-L⓪

Veal

Vitello

V㏒-Tĕ́L-L⓪

POULTRY

Baked chicken

Pollo al forno

POL-LO ahL FOR-NO

Broiled chicken

Pollo alla griglia

POL-LO ahL-Lah GREEL-Yah

Fried chicken

Pollo fritto

POL-LO FREET-TO

Duck

Anitra

ah-NEE-TRah

Turkey

Tacchino

Tah-KEE-NO

Goose

Oca

O-Kah

SEAFOOD

Fish

Pesce

PĔ-SHĔ

Lobster

Aragosta

ah-Rah-GŌS-Tah

Oysters

Ostriche

ŌS-TREE-KĔ

Salmon

Salmone

Sah-L-MŌ-NĔ

Shrimp

Gamberetti

Gah-M-BĔ-RĔT-TEE

Trout

Trota

TRŌ-Tah

Tuna

Tonno

TŌN-NO

OTHER ENTREES

Sandwich

Panino

Pah-NEE-NO

Hot dog

Hot dog

ahT DahG

Hamburger

Hamburger

ahM-Boo-GĕR

French fries

Patatine fritte

Pah-Tah-TEE-Nĕ FREET-Tĕ

Pasta

Pasta

PahS-Tah

Pizza

Pizza

PEET-Sah

VEGETABLES

Carrots
Carote
Kah-RŌ-Tĕ

Corn
Granturco
GRahN-TooR-KO

Mushrooms
Funghi
FooN-GEE

Onions
Cipolle
CHEE-PŌL-Lĕ

Potato
Patate
Pah-Tah-Tĕ

Rice
Riso
REE-ZO

Tomato
pomodoro
PO-MO-DŌ-RO

FRUITS

Apple

Crostata di mela

KROS-Tah'-Tah DEE Mĕ'-Lah

Banana

Banana

Bah-Nah'-Nah

Grapes

Uva

oo'-Vah

Lemon

con limone

KON LEE-MO'-Nĕ

Orange

Succo di arancia

TSoo'-KO DEE ah-Rah'N-CHah

Strawberry

Fragola

FRah'-GO-Lah

Watermelon

Anguria

ahN-Goo'-REE-ah

DESSERT

Desserts
Dolci
DOL-CHEE

Apple pie
Crostata di mela
KROS-Tah-Tah DEE MĕL-Lah

Cherry pie
Crostata di ciliege
KROS-Tah-Tah DEE CHEEL-Yĕ-Jĕ

Pastries
Pasticcini
Pah S-TEE-CHEE-NEE

Candy
Caramella
Kah-Rah-MĕL-Lah

Ice cream
Gelato
Jĕ-Lah-TO

Ice cream cone

Cono di gelato

KO'-NO DEE Jĕ-Lah'-TO

Chocolate

Cioccolata

CHOK-KO-Lah'-Tah

Strawberry

Fragola

FRah'-GO-Lah

Vanilla

Vaniglia

Vah-NEEL-Yah

CONDIMENTS

Salt
Sale
Sᵃʰ-Lĕ

Pepper
Pepe
Pĕ-Pĕ

Sugar
zucchero
TSᵒᵒ-Kĕ-Rᴼ

Mayonnaise
Maionese
Mᵃʰ-Yᴼ-Nĕ-Sĕ

Butter
burro
Bᵒᵒ-Rᴼ

Mustard
Senape
Sĕ-Nᵃʰ-Pĕ

Ketchup
Ketchup
Kĕ-CHᵒᵒP

Vinegar and oil
Aceto e olio
ᵃʰ-CHĕ-Tᴼ   ĕ   ᴼL-Yᴼ

SETTINGS

A cup

Una tazza

OO-Nah Tah-TSah

A glass

Vorrei un bicchiere di...

VO-Bĕ-EE OON BEEK-Yĕ-Bĕ DEE...

A spoon

Un cucchiaio

OON KOOK-Yah-YO

A fork

Una forchetta

OO-Nah FOB-KĕT-Tah

A knife

Un coltello

OON KOL-Tĕl-LO

A plate

Un piatto

OON PEE-ah-T-TO

A napkin

Un tovagliolo

OON TO-Vah-L-YO-LO

HOW DO YOU WANT IT COOKED?

Baked
Al forno
ⓐhL FⓄʹB-NⓄ

Steamed
Al vapore
ⓐhL Vⓐh-PⓄʹ-Bё

Fried
Fritte
FBⒺⒺʹT-Tё

Rare
Al sangue
ⓐhL SⓐhʹN-GWё

Medium
Cotta normale
KⓄʹT-Tⓐh NⓄB-Mⓐh-Lё

Well done
Ben cotta
BёN KⓄʹT-Tⓐh

PROBLEMS

I didn't order this

Non ho ordinato questo

NON O
OR-DEE-Nah-TO KWēS-TO

Is the bill correct?

Il conto è esatto?

EEL KON-TO ē ē-Zah'T-TO

Bring me...

Per favore, mi porti...

PēR Fah-VO'-Rē MEE POR-TEE

another spoon please

Un altro cucchiaio, per piacere

OON ah'L-TRO KOOK-Yah'-YO PF

another fork please

Un' altra forchetta, per piacere

OON ah'L-TRah FOR-Kē'T-Tah PF

another plate please

Un altro piatto, per favore

OON ah'L-TRO PEE-ah'T-TO PF

SHOPPING

Whether you plan a major shopping spree or just need to purchase some basic necessities, the following information is useful.

- Shops are usually open between 9 a.m. and 6 p.m., closing 2 to 3 hours in the afternoon.

- On Saturday most shops close around 1 P.M.

- You are likely to encounter an item called VAT, (value added tax) on purchases. Fortunately, many countries return this tax upon departure. Some customs officials insist on see the merchandise, so keep it together, in carry-on luggage, if possible.

- Always keep receipts for everything you buy!

SIGNS TO LOOK FOR:

FIORAIO (FLORIST)

LIBRERIA (BOOKSTORE)

FARMACIA (PHARMACY)

SUPERMERCATO (SUPERMARKET)

GIOIELLERIA (JEWELRY STORE)

KEY WORDS

Credit card

Carta di credito

KahR-Tah DEE KRĕ-DEE-TO

Money

Denaro

Dĕ-Nah-RO

Receipt

ricevuta

REE-CHĕ-Voo-Tah

Sale

Vendita

'Vĕ'N-DEE-Tah

Store

Negozio

Nĕ-GO'-TSEE-O

Travelers' checks

Travelers check

TRah-Vĕ-LĕRS CHĕK

USEFUL PHRASES

Do you sell...?
Vende...?
VĕN-Dĕ

Do you have...?
Avete...?
ah-Vĕ-Tĕ...

I want to buy...
Vorrei comprare...
VO-Rĕ-EE KOM-PRah-Rĕ...

How much?
Quanto costa?
KWahN-TO KOS-Tah

No thank you
No, grazie
NO GRah-TSEE

I´m just looking
Sto solo guardando
STO SO-LO GWahR-DahN-DO

It's very expensive

E'Molto costoso

ĕ MÓL-TO KOS-TÓ-ZO

Can't you give me a discount?

Potrebbe farmi uno sconto?

PO-TRĔB-Bĕ Fah R-MEE

OO-NO SKON-TO

I'll take it!

Lo prendo!

LO PRĔN-DO

I'd like a receipt please

Vorrei la ricevuta, per favore

VO-RĕE-EE Lah REE-CHĕ-VOO-Tah PF

I want to return this

Vorrei restituire questo

VO-RĕE-EE RĔS-TEE-TOO-EE-Rĕ

KWĕS-TO

It doesn't fit

Non è della mia misura

NON ĕ DĔL-Lah MEE-ah

MEE-SOO-Rah

PHRASEMAKER

I'm looking for...

Sto cercando...

STⓄ CHⒺB-KⓐⓃN-DⓄ...

a bakery

una panetteria

ⓄⓄ-Nⓐ Pⓐ-NⒺT-TⒺ-BⒺⒺ-ⓐ

a bank

una banca

ⓄⓄ-Nⓐ Bⓐ-N-Kⓐ

a barber shop

un barbiere

ⓄⓄ-Nⓐ Bⓐ-B-BⒺⒺ-Ⓔ-BⒺ

a book store

una libreria

ⓄⓄ-Nⓐ LⒺⒺ-BBⒺ-BⒺⒺ-ⓐ

a camera shop

un negozio di macchine fotografiche

ⓄN NⒺ-GⓄ-TSⒺⒺ-Ⓞ DⒺⒺ
Mⓐ-KⒺⒺ-NⒺ FⓄ-TⓄ-GBⓐ-FⒺⒺ-KⒺ

a florist shop

un fiorista

OON FEE-O-REES-Tah

a hair salon

un parrucchiere

OON Pah-ROOK-KEE-ě-Rě

a pharmacy

una farmacia

OO-Nah FahR-Mah-CHEE-ah

PHRASEMAKER

Do you sell...
Vende...
VⒺN-DⒺ

aspirin?
aspirina?
ⓐhS-PⒺⒺ-RⒺⒺ-Nⓐh

cigarettes?
sigarette?
SⒺⒺ-Gⓐh-RⒺT-TⒺ

dresses?
abiti da donna?
ⓐh-BⒺⒺ-TⒺⒺ
Dⓐh DⓄN-Nⓐh

shirts?
camicie?
Kⓐh-MⒺⒺ-CHⒺ

deodorant?
deodorante?
DⒺ-Ⓞ-DⓄ-RⓐhN-TⒺ

film?
rullini fotografici?
RⓄⓄL-LⒺⒺ-NⒺⒺ
FⓄ-TⓄ-GRⓐh-FⒺⒺ-CHⒺⒺ

pantyhose?

collant?

KOL-LahNT

razor blades?

lamette?

Lah-MёT-Tё

shaving cream?

crema da barba?

KRё-Mah Dah BahB-Bah

soap?

di sapone

DEE Sah-PO-Nё

shampoo?

Shampoo?

SHahM-PO

sunglasses?

occhiali da sole?

OK-KEE-ah-LEE Dah SO-Lё

sunscreen?

crema antisolare?

KRё-Mah ahN-TEE-SO-Lah-Rё

HEALTH

Hopefully you will not need medical attention on your trip. If you do, it is important to communicate basic information regarding your condition.

- Check with your insurance company before leaving home to find out if you are covered in a foreign country.

- Have your prescriptions translated before you leave home.

- Take a small first aid kit with you. Include Band Aids, aspirin, cough syrup, throat lozenges, and vitamins.

- Your Embassy or Consulate should be able to assist you in finding health care.

KEY WORDS

Ambulance
Un ambulanza

ⓄⓄN ⓐⓗM-Bⓞⓞ-Lⓐⓗ'N-TSⓐⓗ

Dentist
Un dentista

ⓄⓄN Dⓔ̈N-Tⓔⓔ'S-Tⓐⓗ

Doctor
Un medico

ⓄⓄN Mⓔ̈'-Dⓔⓔ-Kⓞ

Emergency!
Emergenza!

ⓔ̈-Mⓔ̈R-Jⓔ̈'N-TSⓐⓗ

Hospital
Un hospedale

ⓄⓄN Ⓞ'S-Pⓔ̈-Dⓐⓗ'-Lⓔ̈

Prescription
Una ricetta

ⓄⓄ'-Nⓐⓗ Rⓔⓔ-CHⓔ̈'T-Tⓐⓗ

USEFUL PHRASES

I am sick

Sono ammalato

SO'-NO   ahM-Mah-Lah-TO

I need a doctor

Ho bisogno di un dottore

O   BEE-ZON-YO   DEE
OON   DOT-TO'-RE

It's an emergency!

E un'emergenza

A   OON   e-MER-JEN-Sah

Where is the nearest hospital?

Dov'è l'ospedale più vicino?

DO-VE'   LOS-PE-Dah-LE
PEE-OO'   VEE-CHEE-NO

Call an ambulance!

Chiamate un' ambulanza.!

KEE-ah-Mah-TE
OON   ahM-BOO-Lah'N-TSah

I'm allergic to...

Sono allergico a...

SŌ-NO ⓐhL-LĒR-JĒĒ-KO ⓐh...

I'm pregnant

Sono incinta

SŌ-NO ĒĒN-CHĒĒN-Tⓐh

I'm diabetic

Sono diabetico (male)
Sono diabetica (female)

SŌ-NO DĒĒ-ⓐh-BĔ-TĒĒ-KO

SŌ-NO DĒĒ-ⓐh-BĔ-TĒĒ-Kⓐh

I have a heart condition

Sono debole di cuore

SŌ-NO DĔ-BO-LĔ DĒĒ KWŌ-RĔ

I have high blood pressure

Ho la pressione alta

O Lⓐh PRĔS-SĒĒ-Ō-NĔ ⓐhL-Tⓐh

I have low blood pressure

Ho la pressione bassa

O Lⓐh PRĔS-SĒĒ-Ō-NĔ

Bⓐh'S-Sⓐh

PHRASEMAKER

I need...

Ho bisogno di...

Ⓞ Bⓔⓔ-Zⓞ́N-Yⓞ Dⓔⓔ...

a doctor

un medico

ⓞⓞN Mⓔ̆́-Dⓔⓔ-Kⓞ

a dentist

un dentista

ⓞⓞN Dⓔ̆N-Tⓔⓔ́S-Tⓐⓗ

a nurse

un' infermiera

ⓞⓞN ⓔⓔN-Fⓔ̆R-Mⓔⓔ-ⓔ̆́-Rⓐⓗ

an optician

un ottico

ⓞⓞN Ⓞ́T-Tⓔⓔ-Kⓞ

a pharmacist

un farmacista

ⓞⓞN FⓐⓗR-Mⓐⓗ-CHⓔⓔ́S-Tⓐⓗ

PHRASEMAKER
(AT THE PHARMACY)

Do you have...?
Avete...

ⓐh-Vⓔ́-Tⓔ...

aspirin?
aspirina?

ⓐhS-Pⓔⓔ-Rⓔⓔ́-Nⓐh

band aids?
cerotti?

CHⓔ̃-Rⓞ́T-Tⓔⓔ

cough medicine?
sciroppo per la tosse?

CHⓔⓔ-Rⓞ́P-Pⓞ Pⓔ̃R Lⓐh Tⓞ́S-Sⓔ̃

ear drops?
gocce per le orecchi

Gⓞ́-CHⓔ̃ Pⓔ̃R Lⓔ̃ ⓞ-Rⓔ̃-Kⓔⓔ

eye drops?
collirio?

KⓞL-Lⓔⓔ-Rⓔⓔ́-ⓞ

GENERAL INFORMATION

THE DAYS

Monday
Lunedí
L00-Nĕ-DEE´

Tuesday
Martedí
Mah-R-Tĕ-DEE

Wednesday
Mercoledí
Mĕ-R-KO-L-ĕ-DEE´

Thursday
Giovedí
J0-V-ĕ-DEE´

Friday
Venerdí
Vĕ-Nĕ-R-DEE´

Saturday
Sabato
Sah´-Bah-T0

Sunday
Domenica
D0-Mĕ´-NEE-Kah

THE MONTHS

January	February
Gennaio	Febbraio
JĕN-Nah´-YO	FĕB-BRah´-YO

March	April
Marzo	Aprile
Mah´B-TSO	ah-PREE´-Lĕ

May	June
Maggio	Giugno
Mah´-JO	JooN-YO

July	August
Luglio	Agosto
Loo´L-YO	ah-GO´S-TO

September	October
Settembre	Ottobre
SĕT-Tĕ´M-BRĕ	OT-TO´-BRĕ

November	December
Novembre	Dicembre
NO-Vĕ´M-BRĕ	DEE-CHĕ´M-BRĕ

THE SEASONS

Spring

La primavera

Lah PREE-Mah-Vě-Rah

Summer

L'estate

Lě-S-Tah-Tě

Autumn

L'autunno

Low-Toon-No

Winter

L'inverno

Leen-Vě-R-No

NUMBERS

0	1	2
zero	uno	due
TSĕ́-RO	oͦó-NO	Doͦó-ĕ

3	4	5
tre	quattro	cinque
TRĕ	KWah́T-TRO	CHEÉN-KWĕ

6	7	8
sei	sette	otto
Sĕ	Sĕ́T-Tĕ	ÓT-TO

9	10	11
nove	dieci	undici
NO-Vĕ	DEE-ĕ́-CHEE	ooN-DEÉ-CHEE

12	13
dodici	tredici
DO-DEÉ-CHEE	TRĕ-DEÉ-CHEE

14	15
quattordici	quindici
KWah́T-TOR-DEÉ-CHEE	KWEÉN-DEE-CHEE

16	17
sedici	diciassette
Sĕ-DEÉ-CHEE	DEE-CHah́S-Sĕ́T-Tĕ

18

diciotto

DĒ-CHŌT-TŌ

19

diciannove

DĒ-CHⓐN-NŌ-Vⓔ

20

venti

Vⓔ́N-Tēē

30

trenta

TRⓔ́N-Tⓐh

40

quaranta

KWⓐh-Rⓐ́N-Tⓐh

50

cinquanta

CHEⓔN-KWⓐ́N-Tⓐh

100

cento

CHⓔ́N-TŌ

1000

mille

MĒL-Lⓔ

1,000,000

milione

MĒL-YṒ-Nⓔ

COLORS

Black
Nero
Nē´-RO

Blue
Blu
BL⊕

Brown
Marrone
Mₐₕ-RO´-Nē

Gold
Oro
O´-RO

Gray
Grigio
GREE´-JO

Green
Verde
Vēℝ-Dē

Orange

Arancione

ah-Rah-N-CHO-Nĕ

Pink

Rosa

RO-Sah

Purple

Porpora

POR-PO-Rah

Red

Rosso

ROS-SO

White

Bianco

BEE-ah'N-KO

Yellow

Giallo

GEE-ah'L-LO

DICTIONARY

Adjectives are shown in their masculine form, as common practice dictates.

Each English entry is followed by the Italian spelling and the EPLS spelling.

A

a, an un, uno ooN oo-NO

a lot molto MOL-TO

able (to be) potére PO-T(e)-R(e)

above sopra SO-PRah

accident incidente (e)N-CH(ee)-D(e)N-T(e)

accommodation sistemazione S(ee)S-T(e)-Mah-TS(ee)-O-N(e)

account conto KON-TO

address indirizzo (e)N-D(ee)-R(ee)T-TSO

admission ingresso (e)N-GR(e)S-SO

afraid (to be) aver paura ah-V(e)R Pah-oo-Rah

after dopo DO-PO

afternoon pomeriggio PO-M(e)-R(ee)-JO

agency agenzia ah-J(e)N-TS(ee)-Yah

air conditioning aria condizionata
ah-R(ee)-ah KON-D(ee)-TS(ee)-O-Nah-Tah

aircraft aereo ah-(e)-R(e)-O

airline compagnia aerea KOM-Pah-N(ee)-ah ah-(e)-R(e)-ah

airport aeroporto ah-(e)-RO-POR-TO

aisle corridoio KO-R(ee)-DO-(ee)-O

all tutto Too T-TO

almost quasi KWah-Z(ee)

alone solo SO-LO

also anche ah N-K(e)

always sempre S(e)M-PR(e)

ambulance ambulanza ah M-Boo-Lah N-TSah

American americano ah-Mĕ-RĒ-Kah-NŌ

and e ĕ

another un altro ōōN ahL-TRŌ

anything qualsiasi cosa KWahL-SĒ-ah-SĒ KŌ-Sah

apartment appartamento ahP-PahR-Tah-MĕN-TŌ

appetizers antipasti ahN-TĒ-PahS-TĒ

apple mela Mĕ-Lah

appointment appuntamento ahP-PōōN-Tah-MĕN-TŌ

April aprile ah-PRĒ-Lĕ

arrival arrivo ah-RĒ-VŌ

arrive (to) arrivare ah-RĒ-Vah-Rĕ

ashtray portacenere PŌR-Tah-CHĕ-Nĕ-Rĕ

aspirin aspirina ahS-PĒ-RĒ-Nah

attention attenzione ahT-TĕN-TSĒ-Ō-Nĕ

August agosto ah-GŌS-TŌ

author autore ōw-TŌ-Rĕ

automobile macchina Mah-KĒ-Nah

Autumn autunno ōw-TōōN-NŌ

avenue corso KŌR-SŌ

awful terribile TĕR-RĒ-BĒ-LĕY

B

baby bambino BahM-BĒ-NŌ

babysitter babysitter Bĕ-BĒ-SĒ-TĕR

bacon pancetta PahN-CHĕT-Tah

bad cattivo KahT-TĒ-VŌ

bag borsa BŌR-Sah

baggage bagaglio Bah-Gahl-YŌ

baked al forno ahL FŌR-NŌ

bakery fornaio FŌR-Nah-ĒĒ-Ō

banana banana Bah-Nah-Nah

bandage benda BĕN-Dah

bank banca BAN-Kah

barber shop barbiere BAR-BEE-E-RE

bartender barista BA-REES-Tah

bath bagno BAN-YO

bathing suit costume da bagno KOS-TOO-ME Dah
    BAN-YO

bathroom bagno BAN-YO

battery batteria BAT-TE-REE-ah

beach spiaggia SPEE-ah-Jah

beautiful bellissimo BEL-LEES-SEE-MO

beauty shop salone di belleza SAH-LO-NE DEE
BEL-LET-Sah

bed letto LET-TO

beef manzo MAN-TSO

beer birra BEE-Rah

bellman fattorino FAT-TO-REE-NO

belt cintura CHEEN-TOO-Rah

big grande GRAN-DE

bill conto KON-TO

black nero NE-RO

blanket coperta KO-PER-Tah

blue blu BLOO

boat barca BAR-Kah

book libro LEE-BRO

book store libreria LEE-BRE-REE-ah

border confine KON-FEE-NE

boy ragazzo RAH-GAT-TSO

bracelet bracciale BRAH-CHEE-ah-LE

brakes freni FRE-NEE

bread pane PAH-NE

breakfast colazione KO-LAH-TSEE-O-NE

broiled alla griglia ⓐL-Lⓐ GRⒺL-Yⓐ

brown marrone Mⓐ-Rⓞ-Nⓔ

brush spazzola SPⓐT-TSⓄ-Lⓐ

building edificio ⓔ-Dⓔⓔ-Fⓔⓔ-CHⓄ

bus autobus ⓞⓦ-TⓄ-BⓞⓞS

bus station stazione degli autobus STⓐ-TSⒺⒺ-Ⓞ-Nⓔ DⓔL-Yⓔⓔ ⓞⓦ-TⓄ-BⓞⓞS

bus stop fermata dell' autobus FⒺR-Mⓐ-Tⓐ DⓔL ⓞⓦ-TⓄ-BⓞⓞS

business affari ⓐF-Fⓐ-RⒺⒺ

butter burro Bⓞⓞ-RⓄ

buy (to) comprare KⓄM-PRⓐ-Rⓔ

C

cab taxi TⓐK-Sⓔⓔ

call (to) chiamare Kⓔⓔ-ⓐ-Mⓐ-Rⓔ

camera macchina fotografica Mⓐ-Kⓔⓔ-Nⓐ FⓄ-TⓄ-GRⓐ-Fⓔⓔ-Kⓐ

candy caramella Kⓐ-Rⓐ-MⓔL-Lⓐ

car auto ⓐ-ⓞⓞ-TⓄ

carrot carota Kⓐ-RⓄ-Tⓐ

castle castello KⓐS-TⓔL-LⓄ

cathedral cattedrale Kⓐ-Tⓔ-DRⓐ-Lⓔ

celebration celebrazione CHⓔ-Lⓔ-BRⓐ-TSⓔⓔ-Ⓞ-Nⓔ

center centro CHⓔN-TRⓄ

cereal cereali CHⓔ-Rⓔ-ⓐ-Lⓔⓔ

chair sedia Sⓔ-Dⓔⓔ-ⓐ

champagne champagne SHⓐM-PⓐN-Yⓐ

change (exact) resto Rⓔ S-TⓄ

change (to) cambiare KⓐM-Bⓔⓔ-ⓐ-Rⓔ

cheap a buon mercato ⓐ BWⓄN MⒺR-Kⓐ-TⓄ

check (bill in a restaurant) conto KⓄN-TⓄ

cheers salute S(ah)-L(oo)-T(e)

cheese formaggio F(o)R-M(ah)-J(o)

chicken pollo P(o)L-L(o)

child bambino B(ah)M-B(ee)-N(o)

chocolate (flavor) cioccolata CH(o)K-K(o)-L(ah)-T(ah)

church chiesa K(ee)-(e)-S(ah)

cigar sigaro S(ee)-G(ah)-R(o)

cigarettes sigarette S(ee)-G(ah)-R(e)T-T(e)

city citta CH(ee)T-T(ah)

clean pulito P(oo)-L(ee)-T(o)

close (to) chiudere K(ee)-(oo)-D(e)-R(e)

closed chiuso K(ee)-(oo)-Z(o)

clothes vestiti V(e)S-T(ee)-T(ee)

cocktail cocktail K(o)K-T(o)L

coffee caffé K(ah)-F(e)

cold (temperture) freddo FR(e)D-D(o)

comb pettine P(e)T-T(ee)-N(e)

come (to) venire V(e)-N(ee)-R(e)

company (business) ditta D(ee)T-T(ah)

computer calcolatore K(ah)L-K(o)-L(ah)-T(o)-R(e)

concert concerto K(o)N-CH(e)R-T(o)

conference conferenza K(o)N-F(e)-R(e)N-TS(ah)

conference room sala conferenze S(ah)-L(ah)
K(o)N-F(e)-R(e)N-TS(e)

congratulations congratulazioni
K(o)N-GR(ah)-T(oo)-L(ah)-TS(ee)-(o)-N(ee)

copy machine fotocopiatrice F(o)-T(o)-K(o)-P(ee)-(ah)-TR(ee)-CH(e)

corn granturco GR(ah)N-T(oo)R-K(o)

cough la tosse L(ah) T(o)S-S(e)

cover charge coperto K(o)-P(e)R-T(o)

crab granchi GR(ah)N-K(ee)

cream crema KRE-Mah

credit card carta di credito KahR-Tah DE KRE-DE-TO

cup tazza Tah-TSah

customs dogana DO-Gah-Nah

D

dance (to) ballare BahL-Lah-RE

dangerous pericoloso PE-RE-KO-LO-SO

date (calendar) data Dah-Tah

day giorno JE-OR-NO

December dicembre DE-CHEM-BRE

delicious delizioso DO-LE-TSE-O-SO

delighted lietissimo LE-E-TE-SE-MO

dentist dentista DEN-TES-Tah

deodorant deodorante DE-O-DO-Rah N-TE

department store grande magazzino GRah N-DE Mah-Gah-TSE-NO

departure partenza PahR-TEN-TSah

dessert dolce DOL-CHE

detour deviazione DE-VE-ah-TSE-O-NE

diabetic diabetico DE-ah-BE-TE-KO

diarrhea diarrea DE-ah-RE-ah

dictionary dizionario DE-TSE-O-Nah-RE-O

dinner cena CHE-Nah

dinning room sala da pranzo Sah-Lah Dah PRah N-TSO

directions indicazioni EN-DE-Kah-TSE-O-NE

dirty sporco SPOR-KO

disabled invalido EN-Vah-LE-DO

discount sconto SKON-TO

distance distanza DES-Tah N-TSah

doctor dottore DOT-TO-RE

document documento DO-Koo-MEN-TO

dollar dollaro DOL-Lah-RO

down giú Joo

downtown in centro EEN CHeN-TRO

dress vestito VeS-TEE-TO

drink (to) bere Be-Re

drive (to) guidare GWEE-Dah-Re

drugstore farmacia FahR-Mah-CHEE-ah

dry cleaner lavanderia a secco Lah-VahN-Deh-REE-ah ah SeK-KO

duck anitra ah-NEE-TRah

E

ear drops gocce per le orecchie GO-CHe PeR Le O-Re-KEE-e

ear orecchio O-Re-KEE-O

early presto PReS-TO

east est eST

easy facile Fah-CHEE-Le

eat(to) mangiare MahN-Jah-Re

eggs (fried) uova fritte WO-Vah FREET-Te

eggs (scrambled) uova strapazzate WO-Vah STRah-Pah-TSah-Te

egg uovo WO-VO

electricity elettricitá e-LeT-TREE-CHEE-Tah

elevator ascensore ah-SHeN-SO-Re

embassy ambasciata ahM-Bah-SHah-Tah

emergency emergenza e-MeR-JeN-TSah

English inglese EEN-GLe-Ze

enough basta Bah'S-Tah

entrance ingresso EEN-GReS-SO

envelope busta Boo'S-Tah

evening sera Se-Rah

everything tutto TOOT-TO

excellent eccellente E-CHEL-LEN-TE

excuse me mi scusi MEE SKOO-ZEE

exit uscita OO-SHEE-Tah

expensive caro Kah-RO

eye drops gocce per gli occhi GO-CHE PER LYEE OK-KEE

eyes occhi OK-KEE

F

face faccia Fah-CHah

far lontano LON-Tah-NO

fare (cost) costo KOS-TO

fast veloce VE-LO-CHE

fax machine macchina per fax Mah-KEE-Nah PER Fah KS

February febbraio FEB-BRah-YO

few alcuni ahL-KOO-NEE

film (for a camera) rullino ROOL-LEE-NO

fine (very well) bene BE-NE

finger dito DEE-TO

fingernail unghia OON-GEE-ah

fire extinguisher estintore ES-TEEN-TO-RE

fire fuoco FWO-KO

first primo PREE-MO

fish pesce PE-SHE

fit (to) andare bene ahN-Dah-RE BE-NE

flight volo VO-LO

floor (story) piano PEE-ah-NO

florist shop fiorista FEE-O-REES-Tah

flower fiore FEE-O-RE

food cibo CHEE-BO

foot piede PEE-E-DE

fork forchetta FOR-KĕT-Tah

french fries patatine fritte Pah-Tah-TEE-Nĕ FRĔT-Tĕ

fresh fresco FRĕS-KO

Friday venerdi Vĕ-NĕR-DEE

fried fritto FRĔT-TO

friend amico ahM-EE-KO

fruit frutta FRooT-Tah

funny divertente DEE-VĕR-TĕN-Tĕ

G

gas station distributore DEES-TREE-Boo-TO-Rĕ

gasoline benzina BĕN-TSEE-Nah

gate cancello Kah-CHĕL-LO

gentleman signore SEEN-YO-Rĕ

gift regalo Rĕ-Gah-LO

girl ragazza Rah-Gah-T-TSah

glass (drinking) bicchiere BEEK-Yĕ-Rĕ

glasses (eye) occhiali OK-KEE-ah-LEE

gloves guanti GWah-N-TEE

go forza FOR-TSah

gold oro O-RO

golf course campo da golf Kah-M-PO Dah GOLF

golf golf GOLF

good buono BWO-NO

goodbye arrivederci ah-REE-Vĕ-DĕR-CHEE

goose oca O-Kah

grapes uva oo-Vah

grateful grato GRah-TO

gray grigio GREE-JO

green verde VĕR-Dĕ

grocery store drogheria DRO-Gĕ-REE-ah

group gruppo GRooP-PO

guide guida GWEE-Dah
H
hair capelli Kah-PEL-LEE
hairbrush spazzola SPaT-TSO-Lah
haircut taglio di capelli TaL-YO DEE Kah-PEL-LEE
ham prosciutto PRO-SHOOT-TO
hamburger hamburger ahM-BOOR-GER
hand mano Mah-NO
happy felice / contento FE-LEE-CHE / KON-TEN-TO
have, I ho O
he lui LOO-EE
head testa TES-Tah
headache mal di testa MahL DEE TES-Tah
health club club ginnico KLOOB JEN-NEE-KO
heart condition debole di cuore DE-BO-LE DEE KWO-RE
heart cuore KWO-RE
heat calore Kah-LO-RE
hello ciao CHow
help! aiuto ah-YOO-TO
here qui KWEE
holiday festa FES-Tah
hospital ospedale OS-PE-Dah-LE
hot dog hot dog ahT DahG
hotel hotel O-TEL
hour ora O-Rah
how come KO-ME
hurry (to) sbrigarsi ZBREE-Gah-R-SEE
I
I io EE-O
ice cream gelato JE-Lah-TO

ice cubes cubetti di ghiaccio KOO-BĔT-TEE DEE GEE-ah-CHO

ice ghiaccio GEE-ah-CHO

ill ammalato ahM-Mah-Lah-TO

important importante EEM-POR-TahN-TĔ

indigestion l'indigestione EEN-DEE-JĔS-TEE-O-NĔ

information informazione EEN-FOR-Mah-TSEE-O-NĔ

inn albergo ahL-BĔR-GO

interpreter interprete EEN-TĔR-PRĔ-TĔ

J

jacket giubbotto JOO-BŎT-TO

jam marmellata MahR-MĔL-Lah-Tah

January gennaio JĔN-Nah-YO

jewelry gioielli JO-YĔL-LEE

jewelry store gioielleria JO-YĔL-LĔ-REE-ah

job lavoro Lah-VO-RO

juice succo SOOK-KO

July luglio LOOL-YO

June giugno JOON-YO

K

ketchup ketchup KĔ-CHOOP

key chiave KEE-ah-VĔ

kiss bacio Bah-CHO

knife coltello KOL-TĔL-LO

know, I sapere Sah-PĔ-RĔ

L

ladies (restroom) toilette per le donne TWah-LĔT PĔR LĔ DON-NĔ

lady signora SEEN-YO-Rah

lamb agnello ahN-YĔL-LO

language lingua LEEN-GWah

large grande GRⒶN-DⒺ
late tardi TⒶR-DⒺⒺ
laundry lavanderia LⒶ-VⒶN-DⒺ-RⒺⒺ-Ⓐ
lawyer avvocato ⒶV-VⓄ-KⒶ-TⓄ
left (direction) sinistra SⒺⒺ-NⒺⒺS-TRⒶ
leg gamba GⒶM-BⒶ
lemon limone LⒺⒺ-MⓄ-NⒺ
less meno MⒺ-NⓄ
letter lettera LⒺT-TⒺ-RⒶ
lettuce insalata ⒺN-SⒶ-LⒶ-TⒶ
light luce LⓄⓄ-CHⒺ
like, I mi piace MⒺⒺ PⒺⒺ-Ⓐ-CHⒺ
like, I would vorrei VⓄ-RⒺ-ⒺⒺ
lip labbro LⒶB-BRⓄ
lipstick rossetto RⓄS-SⒺT-TⓄ
little piccolo PⒺⒺK-KⓄ-LⓄ
live (to) vivere VⒺⒺ-VⒺ-RⒺ
lobster aragosta Ⓐ-RⒶ-GⓄS-TⒶ
long lungo LⓄⓄN-GⓄ
lost perduto PⒺR-DⓄⓄ-TⓄ
love amore Ⓐ-MⓄ-RⒺ
luck fortuna FⓄR-TⓄⓄ-NⒶ
luggage bagaglio BⒶ-GⒶL-YⓄ
lunch pranzo PRⒶN-TSⓄ
M
maid cameriera KⒶ-MⒺ-RⒺⒺ-Ⓔ-RⒶ
mail posta PⓄS-TⒶ
makeup trucco TRⓄⓄK-KⓄ
man uomo WⓄ-MⓄ
manager direttore DⒺⒺ-RⒺT-TⓄ-RⒺ
map cartina KⒶR-TⒺⒺ-NⒶ

March marzo MAR-TSO

market mercato MER-KAH-TO

matches fiammiferi FEE-ahM-MEE-FE-REE

May maggio MAH-JO

mayonnaise maionese MAH-YO-NE-SE

meal pasto PAHS-TO

meat carne KAHR-NE

mechanic meccanico ME-KAH-NEE-KO

medicine medicina ME-DEE-CHEE-Nah

meeting incontro EN-KON-TRO

Mens (restroom) toilette per uomini TWAH-LET
    PER WO-MEE-NEE

menu menù ME-Noo

message messaggio MES-Sah-JO

milk latte LAHT-TE

mineral water acqua minerale ah-KWah
    MEE-NE-Rah-LE

minute minuto MEE-Noo-TO

Miss signorina SEEN-YO-REE-Nah

mistake sbaglio SBAHL-YO

misunderstanding malinteso MAH-LEEN-TE-SO

moment momento MO-MEN-TO

Monday lunedi Loo-NE-DEE

money soldi SOL-DEE

month mese ME-SE

monument monumento MO-Noo-MEN-TO

more piú PEE-oo

morning mattino MAH-T-TEE-NO

mosque moschea MOS-KE-ah

mother madre MAH-DRE

mountain montagna MON-TahN-Yah

movies film FEELM

Mr. signore SEEN-YO-REE

Mrs. signora SEEN-YO-Rah

much, too molto MOL-TO

museum museo Moo-SEE-O

mushrooms funghi FooN-GEE

music musica Moo-SEE-Kah

mustard senape SEE-Nah-PEE

N

nail polish smalto per le unghie SMah L-TO
    PEER LEE ooN-GEE

name nome NO-MEE

napkin tovagliolo TO-Vah L-YO-LO

near vicino VEE-CHEE-NO

neck collo KOL-LO

need, I ho bisogno O BEE-ZON-YO

never mai Mah-EE

newspaper giornale JOR-Nah-LEE

newstand edicola EE-DEE-KO-Lah

next time la prossima volta Lah PROS-SEE-Mah VOL-Tah

night notte Lah NOT-TEE

nightclub locale notturno LO-Kah-LEE NOT-Too R-NO

no no NO

no smoking non fumatori NON Foo-Mah-TO-REE

noon mezzogiorno MEE-TSO-JOR-NO

north nord NORD

notary notaio NO-Tah-YO

November novembre NO-VEEM-BREE

now adesso ah-DEES-SO

number numero Noo-MEE-RO

nurse infermiera EEN-FEER-MEE-EE-Rah

O

occupied occupato OK-Koo-Pah-TO

ocean oceano O-CHe-ah-NO

October ottobre OT-TO-BRe

officer ufficiale eL ooF-Fee-CHah-Le

oil olio OL-YO

omelet frittata FReeT-Tah-Tah

one way (traffic) senso unico SeN-SO oo-Nee-KO

onions cipolle CHee-POL-Le

open (to) aprire ah-PRee-Re

opera opera O-Pe-Rah

operator centralinista CHeN-TRah-Lee-NeeS-Tah

optician ottico OT-Tee-KO

orange (fruit) arancia ah-Rah N-CHah

order (to) ordinare OR-Dee-Nah-Re

original originale O-Ree-Jee-Nah-Le

owner proprietario PRO-PRee-e-Tah-Ree-O

oysters ostriche OS-TRee-Ke

P

package pacco Pah K-KO

paid pagato Pah-Gah-TO

pain dolore DO-LO-Re

painting dipinto Dee-PeN-TO

pantyhose collant KOL-Lah NT

paper carta Kah R-Tah

park (to) parcheggiare Pah R-Kee-Jah-Re

park parco Pah R-KO

partner (business) socio SO-CHO

party festa Fe S-Tah

passenger passeggero Pah S-Se-Je-RO

passport passaporto Pah S-Sah-POR-TO

pasta pasta PahS-Tah

pastry pasticceria PahS-TEE-CHO-REE-ah

pen penna PEN-Nah

pencil matita Mah-TEE-Tah

pepper pepe PE-PE

perfume profumo PRO-Foo-MO

person persona PER-SO-Nah

person to person diretta con preavviso DEE-RET-Tah
    KON PRE-ah-VEE-ZO

pharmacist un farmacista ON Fah-Mah-CHEES-Tah

pharmacy farmacia Fah-Mah-CHEE-ah

phone book elenco telefonico E-LEN-KO
    TE-LE-FO-NE-KO

photo foto FO-TO

photographer fotografo FO-TO-GRah-FO

pillow cuscino Koo-SHEE-NO

pink rosa RO-Sah

pizza pizza PEET-Sah

plastic plastica PLahS-TEE-Kah

plate piatto PEE-ahT-TO

please per favore / per piacere PER Fah-VO-RE /
    PER PEE-ah-CHE-RE

pleasure piacere PEE-ah-CHE-RE

police polizia PO-LEE-TSEE-ah

police station stazione di polizia STah-TSEE-O-NE DEE
    PO-LEE-TSEE-ah

pork maiale Mah-Yah-LE

porter facchino Fah-KEE-NO

post office ufficio postale oo-FEE-CHO POS-Tah-LE

postcard cartolina Kah R-TO-LEE-Nah

potato patata Pah-Tah-Tah

pregnant incinta ĒN-CHĒN-Tah

prescription ricetta BĒE-CHĒT-Tah

price prezzo PRĒ-TSO

problem problema PRO-BLĒ-Mah

profession professione PRO-FĒS-SĒE-O-NĒ

public pubblico POOB-BLĒE-KO

public telephone telefono pubblico TĒ-LĒ-FO-NO
   POOB-BLĒE-KO

puriified purificata POO-RĒE-FĒE-Kah-Tah

purple porpora POR-PO-Rah

purse borsetta BOR-SĒT-Tah

Q

quality qualitá KWah-LĒE-Tah

question domanda DO-Mahn-N-Dah

quickly in fretta ĒN FRĒT-Tah

quiet (to be) zitto SĒT-TO

quiet! quieto! KWĒE-Ē-TO

R

radio radio Rah-DĒE-O

railroad ferrovia FĒR-O-VĒE-ah

rain pioggia PĒE-O-Jah

raincoat impermeabile ĒM-PĒR-MĒ-ah-BĒE-LĒ

ramp rampa Rahn-M-Pah

rare (steak) al sangue ahL Sahn-GWĒ

razor blades lamette Lah-MĒT-TĒ

ready pronto PRON-TO

receipt ricevuta BĒE-CHĒ-VOO-Tah

recommend (to) raccomandare Rah-KO-Mahn-Dah-RĒ

red rosso ROS-SO

repeat ripeta BĒE-PĒ-Tah

reservation prenotazione PRĒ-NO-Tah-TSĒE-O-NĒ

restaurant ristorante REES-TO-RahN-TE

return (to come back) ritornare REE-TOR-Nah-RE

return (to give back) restituire RES-TEE-TOO-EE-RE

rice riso REE-ZO

rich ricco REEK-KO

right (correct) giusto JOOS-TO

right (direction) destra DES-TRah

road strada STRah-Dah

room stanza STahN-TSah

round trip andata e ritorno ahN-Dah-Tah E REE-TOR-NO

S

safe (box) cassaforte KahS-Sah-FOR-TE

salad insalata EEN-Sah-Lah-Tah

sale vendita VEN-DEE-Tah

salmon salmone SahL-MON-E

salt sale Sah-LE

sandwich panino Pah-NEE-NO

Saturday sabato Sah-Bah-TO

scissors forbici FOR-BEE-CHEE

sculpture scultura SKOOL-TOO-Rah

seafood pesce PE-SHE

season stagione STah-JO-NE

seat posto POS-TO

secretary segretario SEG-RE-TahR-YO

section sezione SE-TSEE-O-NE

September settembre SET-TEM-BRE

service servizio SER-VEE-TSEE-O

several diversi DEE-VER-SEE

shampoo shampoo SHahM-PO

sheets (on a bed) lenzuola LEN-TSWO-Lah

shirt camicia Kah-MEE-CHah

shoe scarpa SK@R-P@

shoe store negozio di scarpe N@-G@-TS@-@
    D@ SK@R-P@

shop (store) negozio N@-G@-TS@-@

shopping center centro commerciale CH@N-TR@
    K@-M@R-CH@-@-L@

shower doccia D@-CH@

shrimp gamberetti G@M-B@-R@T-T@

sick malato M@-L@-T@

sign (display) cartello K@R-T@L-L@

signature firma F@R-M@

single singolo S@N-G@-L@

sir signore S@N-Y@-R@

sister sorella S@-R@L-L@

size taglia T@L-Y@

skin pelle P@L-L@

skirt gonna G@N-N@

sleeve manica M@N-N@-K@

slowly lentamente L@N-T@-M@N-T@

small piccolo P@K-K@-L@

smile (to) sorridere S@R-R@-D@-R@

smoke (to) fumare F@-M@-R@

soap sapone S@-P@N-@

sock calza K@L-TS@

some qualche KW@L-K@

something qualcosa KW@L-K@-Z@

sometimes a volte @ V@L-T@

soon presto PR@S-T@

sorry (I am) mi dispiace M@ D@S-P@-@-CH@

soup minestra M@-N@S-TR@

south sud S@D

souvenir ricordo BEE-KOR-DO

Spanish spagnolo SPahN-YO-LO

speciality specialitá SPE-CHEE-ah-LEE-Tah

speed velocitá VE-LO-CHEE-Tah

spoon cucchiaio KooK-Yah-YO

sport sport SPORT

Spring primavera Lah PREE-Mah-VE-Rah

stairs scale SKah-LE

stamp francobollo FRahN-KO-BOL-LO

station stazione STah-TSEE-O-NE

steak bistecca BEES-TE-Kah

steamed al vapore ahL Vah-PO-RE

stop! Si fermi! SEE FER-MEE

store negozio NE-GO-TSEE-O

storm temporale TEM-PO-Rah-LE

straight ahead avanti diritto ah-VahN-TEE DEE-REET-TO

strawberry fragola FRah-GO-Lah

street via VEE-ah

string corda KOR-Dah

subway metropolitana ME-TRO-PO-LEE-Tah-Nah

sugar zucchero TSooK-KE-RO

suit (clothes) abito completo ah-BEE-TO KOM-PLE-TO

suitcase valigia Vah-LEE-CHah

summer estate E-STah-TE

sun sole SO-LE

sun tan lotion crema solare KRE-Mah SO-Lah-RE

Sunday domenica DO-ME-NEE-Kah

sunglasses occhiali da sole OK-KEE-ah-LEE Dah SO-LE

supermarket supermercato Soo-PER-MER-Kah-TO

surprise sorpresa SOR-PRE-Zah

sweet dolce DOL-CHE

swim (to) nuotare NWO-Tah-Re

swimming pool piscina PEE-SHEE-Nah

synagogue sinagoga SEE-Nah-GO-Gah

T

table tavola Tah-VO-Lah

tampons tamponi Tah M-PO-NEE

tape (sticky) nastro adesivo Nah S-TRO ah-DE-SEE-VO

tape recorder registratore RE-JEE-STRah-TO-RE

tax imposta EEM-POS-Tah

taxi taxi Tah K-SEE

tea té TE

telegram telegramma TE-LE-GRah M-Mah

telephone telefono TE-LE-FO-NO

television televisione TE-LE-VEE-SEE-O-NE

temperature temperatura TEM-PER-ah-Too-Rah

temple tempio TEM-PEE-O

tennis court campo da tennis EEL Kah M-PO Dah
  TEN-NEES

tennis tennis TEN-NEES

thank you molte grazie MOL-TE GRah-TSEE-E

that quello KWEL-LO

the il, la, lo, i, gli, le   EEL/ Lah/ LO/ EE/ LYEE/ LE

theater teatro TE-ah-TRO

there la Lah

they loro LO-RO

this questo KWES-TO

thread filo FEE-LO

throat gola GO-Lah

Thursday giovedi JO-VE-DEE

ticket biglietto BEE-LEE-E-TO

tie cravatta KRah-Vah T-Tah

time ora Ō-Rah

tip (gratuity**)** mancia Mah'N-CHah

tire gomma GŌM-Mah

tired stanco STah'N-KŌ

toast pane tostato Pah-Nē TŌS-Tah-TŌ

tobacco tabacco Tah-Bah'K-KŌ

today oggi Ō-Jēē

toe dito del piede Dēē-TŌ DēL Pēē-ē-Dē

together insieme ēēN-Sē-ē-Mē

toilet paper carta igienica Kah'R-Tah ēē-Jē-Nē-Kah

toilet toilette / gabinetto TWah-LēT / Gah-Bēē-Nē'T-TŌ

tomato pomodoro PŌ-MŌ-DŌ-RŌ

tomorrow domani DŌ-Mah-Nēē

tooth ache mal di denti MahL Dēē Dē'N-Tēē

toothbrush spazzolino da denti SPah'T-TSŌ-Lēē-NŌ Dah Dē'N-Tēē

toothpaste dentifricio Dē'N-Tēē-FRēē-CHŌ

toothpick stuzzicadenti STōō-TSēē-Kah-Dē'N-Tēē

tour giro Jēē-RŌ

tourist office ufficio del turismo ōō-Fēē-CHŌ DēL Tōō-Rēē'S-MŌ

tourist turista Tōō-Rēē'S-Tah

towel asciugamano ah-SHōō-Gah-Mah-NŌ

train treno TRē-NŌ

travel agency agenzia di viaggio ah-Jē'N-TSēē-Yah Dēē Vēē-ah-JŌ

travelers check travelers check TRah-Vē'L-ēRS CHē'KS

trip viaggio Vēē-ah-JŌ

trousers pantaloni Pah'N-Tah-LŌ-Nēē

trout veritá Vē-Rēē-Tah'

truth verita Vē-Rēē-Tah'

Tuesday martedí M@R-T@-D@@

turkey tacchino T@-K@@-N@

U

umbrella ombrello @M-BR@L-L@

understand (to) capire K@-P@@-R@

underwear mutande M@@-T@N-D@

United States Stati Uniti ST@-T@@ @@-N@@-T@@

university universitá @@-N@@-V@R-S@@-T@

up su S@@

urgent urgente @@R-J@N-T@

V

vacancies (accommodation) stanze libere ST@N-TS@
    L@@-B@-R@

vacant libero L@@-B@-R@

vacation vacanza V@-K@N-TS@

valuable di valore D@@ V@-L@-R@

value valore V@-L@-R@

vanilla vaniglia V@-N@@L-Y@

veal vitello V@@-T@L-L@

vegetables verdura V@R-D@@-R@

view vista V@@S-T@

vinegar aceto @-CH@-T@

voyage viaggio V@@-@-J@

W

waiter cameriere K@-M@-R@@-@-R@

waitress cameriera K@-M@-R@@-@-R@

want, I voglio V@L-Y@

wash (to) lavare L@-V@-R@

watch orologio @-R@-L@-J@

watch out! attenzione! @T-T@N-TS@@-@-N@

water acqua @-KW@

watermelon anguria ahN-GOO-REE-ah

we noi NOY

weather tempo TEM-PO

Wednesday mercoledí MER-KO-LE-DEE

week settimana SET-TEE-Mah-Nah

weekend fine settimana FEE-NE SET-TEE-Mah-Nah

welcome benvenuto BEN-VE-NOO-TO

well done ben cotto BEN KO-TO

west ovest O-VEST

what? cosa? KO-Zah

wheelchair sedia a rotelle SED-Yah ah RO-TEL-LE

when? quando KWahN-DO

where dove DO-VE

which? quale KWah-LE

white bianco BEE-ahN-KO

who chi KEE

why? perché PER-KE

wife moglie MOL-YE

wind vento VEN-TO

window finestra FEE-NES-TRah

wine list lista dei vini LEES-Tah DE VEE-NEE

wine vino VEE-NO

winter inverno EEN-VER-NO

with con KON

woman donna DON-Nah

wonderful meraviglioso ME-Rah-VEEL-YO-SO

world mondo MON-DO

wrong (incorrect) sbagliato SBahL-Yah-TO

YZ

year anno ahN-NO

yellow giallo Jah-L-LO

yes sí SEE
yesterday ieri YE-REE
you tu TOO
zipper cerniera CHER-NEE-E-Rah
zoo zoo TSO-O

INDEX

a, an 29

air travel 46-47

anger words 47

baggage 52-53

breakfast 90

bank 36-39

bus travel 57, 59, 62

car travel 64-65

colors 126-127

days 120

desserts 100

dictionary 128

dining 82

dinner 92

directions 24-25

drinks 86

emergencies 51

endearments 46

entertainment 40-43

epls symbols 7

essential words and phrases 10-51

exclamations 48-49

general information 120

greetings 10-11

hotels 70

introduction 16

lunch 92

medical 114

money 36-37

months 121

numbers 124-125

opposites 44-45

pharmacy 119

post office 34-35

pronunciation guide 6

questions 18-20, 23-25

restaurants 82

rest rooms 25

seasons 122

shopping 106

sightseeing 40-43

subway travel 66

taxis 68-69

telephone 30-33

thanks 154-155

time 26-27

titles 11

train travel 59

travel 52

THANKS!

The nicest thing you can say to anyone, in any language, is thank you. Try some of these languages using the incredible EPLS Vowel Symbol System™.

Spanish GR(ah)-S(EE)-(ah)S	**French** M(ě)R-S(EE)
German D(ah)N-K(uh)	**Italian** GR(ah)T-S(EE)-(ě)
Japanese D(O)-M(O)	**Chinese** SH(A) SH(A)

Swedish	Portuguese
TⓐⓗK	Ⓞ-BⓇⒺⒺ-Gⓐⓗ́-DⓄ

Arabic	Greek
SHⓞⓞ-KⓇⓐⓗN	ⓔF-Hⓐⓗ-ⓇⒺⒺ-STⓄ́

Hebrew	Russian
TⓄ-Dⓐⓗ́	SPⓐⓗ-SⒺⒺ-Bⓐⓗ

Swahili	Romanian
ⓐⓗ-Sⓐⓗ́N-TⒶ	Mⓞⓞ́LT-Sⓞⓞ-Mⓔ̆SK

Tagolog	Hawaiian
Sⓐⓗ-Lⓐⓗ-Mⓐⓗ́T	Mⓐⓗ-Hⓐⓗ́-LⓄ

Order From Your
Local Bookstore Now!

Also Available
Easily Pronounced **SPANISH**
ISBN 0-9728160-0-3

Easily Pronounced **FRENCH**
ISBN 0-9728160-3-8

Easily Pronounced **GERMAN**
ISBN 0-9728160-5-4

Easily Pronounced **ITALIAN**
ISBN 0-9728160-4-6

Easily Pronounced **JAPANESE**
ISBN 0-9728160-6-2

FACIL A   PRONUNCIAR **INGLES**
ISBN 0-9728160-1-1

EPLS Publishing
www.epls.biz
702-387-7220

Printed in the United States
22623LVS00001B/46-63

9 780972 816045